The Early Years
of Charlie Chaplin

The Early Years of Charlie Chaplin

Final Shorts and First Features

Lisa Stein Haven

WHITE
OWL

First published in Great Britain in 2023 by
White Owl
An imprint of
Pen & Sword Books Ltd
Yorkshire – Philadelphia

ISBN 978 1 52678 072 0

A CIP catalogue record for this book is
available from the British Library.

Typeset by Mac Style
Printed in the UK by CPI Group (UK) Ltd, Croydon, CR0 4YY.

MIX
Paper | Supporting
responsible forestry
FSC   FSC® C013604
www.fsc.org

Pen & Sword Books Limited incorporates the imprints of Atlas,
Archaeology, Aviation, Discovery, Family History, Fiction, History,
Maritime, Military, Military Classics, Politics, Select, Transport, True
Crime, Air World, Frontline Publishing, Leo Cooper, Remember When,
Seaforth Publishing, The Praetorian Press, Wharncliffe Local History,
Wharncliffe Transport, Wharncliffe True Crime, White Owl and After
the Battle.

For a complete list of Pen & Sword titles please contact

PEN & SWORD BOOKS LIMITED
47 Church Street, Barnsley, South Yorkshire, S70 2AS, England
E-mail: enquiries@pen-and-sword.co.uk
Website: www.pen-and-sword.co.uk

Or

PEN AND SWORD BOOKS
1950 Lawrence Rd, Havertown, PA 19083, USA
E-mail: Uspen-and-sword@casematepublishers.com
Website: www.penandswordbooks.com

This book is dedicated to Kate Guyonvarch, in gratitude for her years of dedication to Sir Charles Chaplin, and support for his many needy scholars and admirers.

Contents

Introduction: The Road to the
First National Contract

Samuel Clemens (AKA Mark Twain) was born on, and died during, rare appearances of Haley's comet. His exceptional life both fulfilled and predicted this noteworthy framing. Similarly, Charles Spencer Chaplin was born at Easter and died on Christmas Day. The only son of Charles Spencer Chaplin, Sr. and Hannah Harriet Pedlingham Hill would live a life of similar magnitude, but instead of excelling at the art of words like Clemens, Chaplin would act as a pioneer of the seventh art, the art of film.

Born on 16 April 1889 on East Lane in the Walworth region of South London, Chaplin's idyllic family life, as he described it, effectively ended with the passing of his third year, when his parents separated. Both parents were in the field of the music hall, with Hannah (stage name Lili Harley) having worked as a soubrette on stage until the infamous night when Charlie, then aged 5, accompanied her to work and, when she lost her voice during her performance, took over for her, singing "E dunno where 'e are,' to great acclaim, thereby giving him an obsession with public performance that would last his whole life long.

Charles Chaplin, Sr. was quite a successful singer during this time, having left a family of publicans to pursue a career onstage. Sheet music adorned with his likeness still exists, for songs such as 'Oui, trés bong', 'The Girl was Young and Pretty', and others, but he had a drink problem that wrecked his career by the time of Charlie's third birthday. Hannah was left on her own with two boys: Sydney John, aged 7 of an unnamed father and Charlie, aged 3. She tried to make ends meet any way she could, sometimes sewing gloves for a small wage. By Charlie's seventh birthday in 1896, Hannah showed her first signs of mental instability and the authorities were forced to have her committed, leaving him alone on the streets because half-brother Sydney was trying to earn a wage for them at sea. In the years before their mother's death, both boys had spent some time at the Lambeth workhouse, where Sydney learned to be a seaman aboard the Exmouth Training Ship, used solely for this purpose. Although being in the workhouse was a source of horror and shame to both boys, this training would prove invaluable to the Chaplin family's later financial struggles, eventually lifting the two boys out of abject poverty.

Although Charlie was probably the first brother to land a decent stage role, in American actor William Gillette's 1905 London run of *Sherlock Holmes*, as Billy the page boy, it was Sydney's luck in achieving a place in Fred Karno's troupe, 'Karno's London Comedians', that would play the biggest role in the brothers' future lives on the stage and later the screen. Karno's Fun Factory on Vaughan Road in Camberwell, South London, was well known as the origination of the slapstick comedy business that later made it into American (Hollywood) films, mainly through the Keystone studios in Glendale, California. Sydney, immediately upon being hired by Karno, was sent to the States (in 1906) for a Karno tour through the American vaudeville houses, mostly in New York and environs. He had chosen to go, because he loved the adventure, but mainly because the overseas troupes earned higher wages. In 1908, after Sydney settled back into touring England, Charlie was hired and, like his brother, very soon went off to America, the first time in 1910 and the second in 1912, a tour which allowed him to see the far reaches of the country, as he played dates as far north as Winnipeg, Canada and as far west as Los Angeles. While in New York on the second tour, Charlie received a cryptic cable from the great Mack Sennett (mistakenly referring to him as 'Chaffin'), offering him a job at his Keystone studio. Charlie left the Karno troupe in Kansas City to join Sennett and never returned to the vaudeville or music hall stage.

Although Sennett was initially displeased with Chaplin's youthful looks, the young Englishman soon proved himself, eventually making thirty-six films with the company, with his last, *His Prehistoric Past*, filmed in December 1914, featuring brother Sydney in the frame story, – Charlie had persuaded Sydney to join him in California earlier that year. Charlie's first film was *Making a Living*, in which he plays a mustachioed con man, but he was to create the beloved Little Tramp character shortly thereafter, a persona he would inhabit in one form or other until after 1940. His first released film in this guise was *Kid Auto Races at Venice*, filmed 7 February 1914, in which the Little Tramp does his best to interrupt a filming of the kiddie soapbox races. The tramp's first actual film (made first, in other words) was *Mabel's Strange Predicament* set in a hotel and starring Mabel Normand as well as many Keystone regulars. Mabel, Henry Lehrman, George Nichols and Sennett himself directed Charlie's films until *Caught in the Rain*, released 4 May 1914, which was the first film directed by Charlie. He would be his own director for the remainder of his career.

At the end of his contract with Keystone in December 1914, Charlie provided his brother Sydney as a sort of swap for himself, because he now wished to make films with another company. Bronco Billy Anderson, the second half of the Essanay company (with George K. Spoor being the first half) talked Charlie into joining Essanay in January, but in Chicago, where the base of operations was located. His contract stipulated $1,250 per week, fifteen films and a $10,000 bonus. Charlie signed, but upon arriving in Chicago was not greeted by Spoor and his entourage at all, because Spoor was not happy with the generous offer Anderson had promised the young star. In fact, he also took his time paying out the $10,000. With its notoriously cold and windy winters – bad weather regularly coming in off of Lake Michigan – Charlie lasted one film, *His New Job,* at the Chicago studios then demanded to go west to the Niles Canyon studios that Anderson had been using for his westerns. Some of his remaining films for Essanay were filmed in Niles, such as *The Champion* and *The Tramp*, but others used locations in San Francisco and Los Angeles instead. Due to the fact that the Essanay films were made and appeared in 1915, the year of 'Chaplinitis' (the great Chaplin craze), Charlie was well aware of his worth by the time the year came to a close. Sydney, by this time, had left Keystone and busied himself with achieving the best possible contract for his brother's next run of films, eventually winning a million-dollar contract for him with Mutual Films and John Freuler. Mutual gave Charlie his own studio on the corner of Lillian Way and Eleanor Avenue, to be called the Lone Star studio.

Charlie noted that the time completing his contract with the Mutual Film Company (1916–1917) were his 'happiest years.' Certainly, most of the twelve films he made with Mutual have stood the test of time and are still considered masterpieces, films like *The Pawnshop*, *The Immigrant*, and *Easy Street*. While Chaplin had played with creating a mixture of comedy and pathos in earlier films like Essanay's *The Bank*, he was able to create more compelling films at Lone Star, some of which, like *Easy Street*, contained thinly veiled social criticism along with its excellent comedy. It was clear by the end of 1917 that Chaplin planned to take greater chances yet but would need the right sort of contract and freedom to do so, one that would allow him to build and reside in his own studio, a studio he actually owned.

Just a few months before signing Chaplin, businessmen Thomas L. Tally and John D. Williams decided to offer Adolph Zukor at Paramount Artcraft some competition where he had previously had none, by forming a production and distribution company they named First National Exhibitor's Circuit. The new company held its first meeting in April 1917 and signed a contract with Chaplin, negotiated again through Charlie's half-brother Syd Chaplin, in June of that year. Having only received one offer, and that from Chaplin's present employer Mutual Films, Syd made the following statement to the press from Chicago:

> There is one thing that will be stipulated in the articles of all Charlie Chaplin contracts hereafter, and that is that Charlie be allowed all the time he needs and all the money for producing them the way he wants ... The settings and stage properties will be the finest. It is quality, not quantity that we are after. After we have made a scene and it isn't up to the new Chaplin quality, it will be made over. And then, if the whole reel doesn't satisfy Charlie, it will not be released, no matter what money is offered, but thrown into the discard where it belongs. (Exhibitor's Trade Review, April 28, 1917)

Indeed, Chaplin would push the contract he did finally receive from First National to the limits of its patience and, arguably, several less-than-quality films were released under its masthead. But his five-year tenure with First National would prove all important to the creation of feature masterpieces to come, such as *The Gold Rush* (1925) (Chaplin's own personal favorite), *The Circus* (1928), *City Lights* (1931), *Modern Times* (1936) and on into the talkies.

Chapter 1

Negotiating with First National, Leaving Mutual Film Corp., Building the Chaplin Studios

Like many of Charlie's most fruitful and important endeavors, the First National contract seemed to come about due to an alignment of the planets, his taking a long jump and landing in a pile of golden mud, pure happenstance, or dumb luck – or, as Carl Jung might even have called it, synchronicity. Though the First National contract would tax Chaplin's creative juices and his patience from time to time, he would come out the other end primed to produce some of his greatest silent features, so it can be argued that the hell he experienced during these years was not for naught. It began with a well-timed business venture on the part of a group of fifty exhibitors who met in New York City at the Astor Hotel on 27 April 1917,[1] while Charlie was working under his Mutual Films contract, making some of the finest of his comedy shorts.

The initial leaders of the First National Exhibitors Circuit, Incorporated were President S. L. Rothapfel, of the Rialto Theatre, New York City, Vice-President T. L. Tally of Tally's Los Angeles, and Secretary-Treasurer Harry Schwalbe, Philadelphia.[2] They hoped to form the first group of state rights buyers and exhibitors whose purpose would be to purchase big feature films (having a start-up purse of $20 million) and the rights to releasing those films throughout the United States and Canada, thereby doing away with the middlemen that heretofore had led to the exorbitant prices exhibitors had to pay to screen such films. Perhaps there was no idea initially of producing films themselves, but this quickly changed as the organization grew and their financial capabilities became greater. J.D. Williams, T. L. Tally again and E. B. Johnston were the initial representatives for the group, meaning that these gentlemen hit the road and spent their time glad-handing, networking and signing up new recruits, i.e., new members, until membership numbers totaled 300 by summer 1917.[3] J.D. Williams dreamed up the initial idea and fleshed it out with Tally's help and so, in addition to representative, was elected manager. Williams, an Aussie, had built the 2,000-seat Lyric Theatre in Sydney in 1909 and forty other community houses since that time, and naturally brought that experience to this venture, as did all the elected officials of the organization. As President Rothapfel remarked following the group's first official meeting:

> The board of directors have been given unlimited power to buy, lease or otherwise procure films on the open market. Once purchased, the film becomes the exclusive property of the circuit. Each member will control the rights to it in his respective territory and can dispose of it as he sees fit.[4]

The group had divided the United States plus Canada into four districts: western, central, Atlantic and southern, with two directors per district, except for the southern, which had only one director, making seven total. Districts were then sub-divided into territories, with Los Angeles falling under the control of T. J. Tally.

The organization succeeded in purchasing its first film from Essanay studios in late spring 1917, entitled *On Trial*, and they were on the way. It was clear that at least Tally, if not the organization, had set a goal of signing Chaplin at the end of his Mutual contract in summer 1917, probably realizing that such a contract, while expensive, would guarantee their survival for many years to come. A profile of Tally published in *The Motion Picture News* in 1914 suggests that he had the perfect skillset for the job. Thomas J. Talley had opened a phonograph parlor in downtown Los Angeles at the turn of the twentieth century, at a time when even sound technology hadn't been properly worked out yet. Intrigued by the concept of the moving picture, Tally was able to acquire one of the first moving picture machines to leave Thomas A. Edison's Orange, New Jersey, laboratories and introduced it to the citizens of Los Angeles. Films got longer and more interesting, but his customers seemed to enjoy the films and the music he provided to them equally. So, according to this account, he decided to combine the two and make the film accompanied by music the main feature in his place, with no room for vaudeville turns of any kind. As the writer William Parker notes, 'this studying of his patrons has become second nature to Tally. The personal equation enters largely into Tally's business and it is responsible for much of his success.'[5] In addition, Tally stuck to this one thing – screening films, and did it the best way it could be done, eventually building a 900-seat Tally's Theatre on Broadway between Seventh and Eighth in downtown LA, with films running continuously from noon to 10.30pm, featuring roomy seats at three different price points to meet demand. He screened the best one-reelers available until he refused to screen shorts at all and moved to top-notch features only, investing in a pipe organ as well as a pit orchestra to accompany them. Finally, as much as Chaplin (Syd Chaplin, that is, who would be negotiating) could appreciate all this attention to detail, it is perhaps Tally's comportment that he could relate to best: 'Tally personally is a man of great energy. He has that nervous restlessness which characterizes almost every successful man. He is full of practical ideas, brief but lucid in his conversation and a shrewd businessman.'[6] And, he would have had to have been with Syd, who now counted this as his third contract negotiation for his brother. Even though the two men resided in California, the negotiations were to take place in New York, the official home of the Circuit offices.

Syd Chaplin and long-time Chaplin lawyer Nathan Burkan took the train to New York in April 1917 to begin negotiations for Charlie's new film contract. Mutual was offering a flat $1 million – truly not a bad offer, but staying with them would mean staying at Lone Star studios, making films in the same manner, and in the same speedy fashion. Chaplin's tenure with Mutual had been a good one, but he wanted to move on to a contract that offered him more independence in one form or another, his ultimate goal being, as his brother had recently mentioned to the press, total independence at some point in the near future.

The shiny new First National Exhibitors Circuit, with all its 'youthful' enthusiasm and growing pot of money might just be the next firm step on the ladder for Charlie Chaplin. T. J. Tally, and America's greatest comedy star. J.D. Williams, were quick to throw their proverbial hats into the Chaplin ring, offering him $1,075,000 and a complicated contract worked out in conjunction with Syd and Burkan by 19 June; back in Hollywood Charlie took his time to pore over it, reading it out loud to himself and finally signing on 18 July.[7] Some of the significant points of the contract included the fact that the length of film footage didn't matter; if the film was crap, it was crap at 2,000ft or 4,000ft in length. It would be scrapped all the same. By the same token, if it was good, it was good no matter the footage and the price would not increase if the footage increased (of course, this was to cause problems later with *The Kid*). Also, as David Robinson notes in his fine biography, Syd mentioned in a letter to Charlie that the First National negotiators were demanding two negatives for every film, and he felt that since they had been so very gracious on other aspects of the contract that this was something easy to give them in return. They even agreed to pay an extra $500 per film for this additional negative. Syd urged Charlie to adopt the use of a third camera on the set as a matter of course from then on: 'I certainly think it is worth the added cost to have a brand new negative locked away for the future, especially as the rights to the pictures revert to you after five years, and I feel sure they have a great future value.'[8]

Chaplin was to deliver eight two-reel films in a year (though reports indicated it was sixteen months) in which he would be the central star. As he reported to the press:

> The members of the Association are certain I will give them my best, for my compensation is on a profit-sharing basis with them. There will be a great incentive for all of us to do our best. The production will depend upon my efforts, and we will work together to make the comedies bigger drawing cards than ever before.[9]

The contract itself contains the following important elements: 1) the first sentence of the paragraph above, 2) Chaplin would rent two negatives and one positive to First National per film, with an option for First National to make more of each if desired, 3) Chaplin grants to First National the sole and exclusive rights license to use, release, distribute and exhibit photoplays (films) upon release worldwide for a period of five years, 4) the title to all negatives and all prints and plates therefrom remain permanently with Chaplin, 5) First National provides a $200,000 signing bonus (which actually ended up being $200,500, $20,000 of which Chaplin didn't have to return if the whole thing fell through), which included $75,000 simply for signing and $125,000 for the eighth film in the contract, which would then would not be paid at the time of delivery. Also, Chaplin would receive $125,000 per reel delivered, with $140,500 for the third reel, if there was one, 6) after termination of the license, First National would return all positive and negative prints to Chaplin for no remuneration, no matter who had made them, and 7) an application for copyright registration in Chaplin's name, as the copyright owner, would be made by First National and sent to Chaplin within ten days after registration. Although Nathan Burkan, Syd and Charlie were happy with this contract at the time, it would prove to be one of the most, if not *the* most, contentious contract of Chaplin's career, as will be apparent from the many confrontations, obfuscations and eventual contract modifications over the five years Chaplin worked to complete it. The industry press noted that his motivations for a contract with a new film company were not totally remunerative:

> What perhaps is a new twist in a motion picture player way, he is concerned about the quality of the pictures with which his name is to be associated. He is ambitious. He is anxious to maintain his grip on the regard of picturegoers, to advance along with the most progressive of producers.[10]

According to one report, at the time of Chaplin's signing of the First National contract, there were no plans to build a studio. In fact, John Jasper and the Lone Star studio Chaplin and company used during the Mutual contract were still considered possibilities for the Chaplin enterprise. Another option under consideration was to simply rent a larger studio.[11] By 2 October, in an article in which he recounted his plans just a week after completing his final Mutual film, *The Adventurer*, which Chaplin claimed to have cut together in one night, on Sunday, 30 September, he announced that two locations were being considered for building a new studio. He planned to spend six weeks' vacation in New York, with the 'motion picture plant' to be built while he was gone, exclaiming to Grace Kingsley that while he had many plans for the space, 'about one thing I am certain – I am going to build a little bungalow, where I can work when the mood strikes me.'[12] Although he would get his bungalow in essence, the studio complex would not be completed by the end of October, but more like the first weeks of 1918.

Lord Northcliffe, the owner of the British newspapers *The Times* and *The Daily Mail* (essentially a tabloid) started a conscription campaign back in 1915 which was only slightly successful. By the summer of 1917, he was resorting to underhanded tactics of one type or another. One underhanded strategy was to dress Charlie Chaplin down for not returning to Britain to serve in the war. Northcliffe wrote:

> Nobody would want Charlie Chaplin to join up if the Army doctors pronounced him unfit, but until he has undergone medical examination he is under the suspicion of regarding himself as specially privileged to escape the common responsibilities of British citizenship. This thought may not have occurred to the much-boomed film performer, and he will no doubt be thankful that an opportunity for reminding him has been presented by the course of events.
>
> Charlie in khaki would be one of the most popular figures in the army. He would compete in popularity even with Bairnsfather's 'Old Bill'. If his condition did not warrant him going into the trenches, he could do admirable work by amusing troops in billets. In any case, it is Charlie's duty to offer himself as a recruit and thus show himself proud of his British origin. It is his example which will count so very much, rather than the difference to the war that his joining up will make. We shall win without Charlie but (his millions of admirers will say) we would rather win with him.[13]

In the months before Chaplin finished up his Mutual contract in September 1917, the Lord Northcliffe smear campaign had taken a firm hold and was causing Chaplin great concern – so great, that he finally registered for the service on 5 June 1917.[14] The Mutual Films contract itself opened him up to this sort of critique because it specified that Chaplin could not leave the United States without the corporation's permission, which, during the war, it was not likely to give. But as Chaplin himself stated in a formal response to Northcliff in the press, the feeling was that Northcliff's bile towards him had more to do with Chaplin's legal stoppage of the publication of a tawdry faux biography in the *Daily Mail* a few months earlier, than the fact that Chaplin wasn't on a battlefield somewhere fighting for his country:

> At one time Lord Northcliffe assumed an entirely different attitude, and one incident that occurred is probably responsible for his change toward me. His papers began printing an unauthorized biography of me. In one article, the author became so personal as to say my father beat my mother. The result was that I stopped further publication of the articles through my lawyers.[15]

Northcliffe's revenge followed hard on this action. The fact that other British media outlets, such as *The Economist*, did not align themselves with Northcliffe's campaign at the time should have given Chaplin some sense of relief but seeing the word 'slacker' attached to his name, even if only in articles that laid out the pros and cons of the situation, as well as receiving the occasional white feather in the mail, had to be disconcerting. Even the British Embassy's public announcement in the press of its support of Chaplin did not make the problem disappear completely:

> Chaplin is considered to have done his share for the moment by subscribing to the British and American war loans and the American Red Cross ... We would not consider [him] a slacker unless we received instructions to put the compulsory service law into effect in the United States and unless, after that, he refused to join the colours.[16]

Indeed, Chaplin was donating large sums of money to the Liberty loan drives – as much as $250,000 in 1917 alone, well before he went along on the Third Liberty Loan drive in April 1918. Although he was doing so mainly to assuage any guilt he might have had about not serving, it was also to demonstrate an alternate sort of patriotism that he hoped would mean something to his public.

The long break in New York, as Grace Kingsley had reported on 2 October, did not happen. Chaplin chose instead to spend about a week in Hawaii, a place he had heard and wondered about, but more importantly, a place that had secured him for the first of what would be many inspiring Liberty Loan speeches. Perhaps with this engagement, secured by the Ad Club of Honolulu, Chaplin found yet another way to combat the negative rhetoric against his lack of war service transmitted globally by Lord Northcliffe and his *Daily Mail.* The Chaplin party consisted of the actor, of course; Tom Harrington, his valet and man Friday; Rob Wagner, writer and noted socialist; and Edna Purviance.

Chaplin's leading lady since the onset of the Essanay contract in 1915, Purviance would continue on in the First National films in that position, although they were destined to be her last save one: Chaplin's first film of his independence, United Artists' *Woman of Paris* (1924). Some have speculated that her inclusion in this party may have been Chaplin's last-ditch effort to see if their previous attempts at an amorous relationship had any chance of a future. With Harrington and especially Wagner aboard however, this seems unlikely, because how much time in a short seven-day trip would he have had to devote to her anyway? The public came out to see Charlie Chaplin, how he would look and act in real life, not to see Edna Purviance. So, her inclusion in the trip remains anomalous.

Rob Wagner might be labeled the same, except that he could be better described as an important socio-political influence on Chaplin, as was most any other person to befriend the young British star at this time. Robert Leicester Wagner (1872–1942) had come to Hollywood in 1906 at the behest of his first wife's doctor. Although she subsequently died there, Wagner and his two sons stayed. He had gained his reputation not as a writer but as an artist/illustrator. His second wife, Florence, suggested, however, that as they were on the cusp of a new and fascinating industry in California, he write about films and filmmakers instead, which soon led to great success. Being a lifelong progressive, Wagner decided in 1929 to launch *Script* magazine, which has been labeled the cultural precursor of the still-flourishing *New Yorker* magazine. It was known for its frank accounts of America's socio-political atmosphere, and featured controversial writers such as William Saroyan, Upton Sinclair and Dalton Trumbo. In addition to the Honolulu 'vacation,' Wagner would accompany Chaplin on his Third Liberty Loan tour around the American South in spring 1918, and give the actor several opportunities to see his own writing published in the 1930s, at the point in Chaplin's life when this became important to him. Despite the twenty-seven-year difference in their ages, Wagner was an important and influential friend to Chaplin for many years. His presence in Honolulu, at Chaplin's first Liberty Loan speech, allows the idea that Wagner may have contributed to Chaplin's involvement in the Liberty Loan movement from the start, and therefore, was instrumental in helping him to both find a way around the bilious Northcliffe rhetoric and to begin to understand where he himself stood as a person and public celebrity on the socio-political spectrum.

The Chaplin party arrived sometime on Wednesday, 10 October 1917 on the SS *Matsonia* in Honolulu, Hawaii.[17] There is no press coverage of the party on 11 October, so perhaps the group were somehow able to escape and enjoy the beach and some actual downtime during this day. By Friday 12 October, Chaplin was visiting Schofield Barracks, seventeen miles outside of Honolulu, an army base actively playing its part in World War I: 'The 9th Field Artillery passed in review complimenting Major Charles Mettler and his guests, among whom was the famous Charlie Chaplin. At 10.00 am, batteries D, E, and F, of the First Field Artillery, gave an exhibition drill in honor of the same party.'[18] The 13 October was also spent quietly, although at least Chaplin and Purviance attended a meal in a private home. Clearly, though, Chaplin wanted to see one of the living volcanoes and they needed to travel to Hilo to achieve that. So, on Sunday 14 October, Chaplin and his party arrived in

Hilo, on the island of Hawaii (the big island), to travel out to Mauna Kea volcano, very active at the time. A small town, Hilo itself and its native Hawaiian and Japanese citizens made a great impression on the Chaplin party. That afternoon, they toured the town on foot, 'with a band of laughing kids on their trail, and in every store they entered, the crowds followed. If ever a popular man entered Hilo, it was Charlie Chaplin.'[19]

Tuesday 16 October was to be the most important of the trip, because Chaplin was scheduled to give his first Liberty Loan speech (the keynote, no less) at the Ad Club luncheon on the roof of the colossal Alexander Young building. It was reported to be the most well-attended Ad Club meeting in some time. After a selection of patriotic songs by the Second Infantry band and a rendition of *Over There* by the Ad Club quartet, the speeches began. After several speeches – by the Chinese representative, the Japanese representative, the female representative, and the Ad Club president, among others – it was finally Chaplin's turn. He climbed on a chair and then up onto a table, then waited for the crowd to quiet down. He began:

This is the first time I have ever made a speech, and naturally, I feel a little diffident. Your chairman has called upon me to speak for the children. I wish I could express the thoughts of the children, but the best that I can say is, let's all buy Liberty bonds, and get it over there.[20]

No Gettysburg address, still, given the rapturous applause that followed, it's clear that Chaplin's brief and pointed message was appreciated following the many long-winded speeches that came before him: 'Charlie hadn't his mustache nor his trick shoes, but he had his gift of walking right into the affections of his audience, and in even greater measure than is shown on the screen in the funniest of his pictures.'[21] Chaplin's duty done, his taste for such public speaking piqued, his First National contract calling, he packed up his three companions and sailed back to Los Angeles the next day, most likely thinking about the possibility of a new studio and all that would entail.

In fact, the very day that Chaplin was giving his first Liberty Loan speechlet, his brother Syd was announcing to the press information about the new studio, that property had been purchased and an architect and design chosen. John Jasper, manager of Chaplin's Lone Star studio, described some of the thinking and negotiating that had gone into this final decision in a 3 July letter to Sydney, who was still in New York. This studio, which Chaplin had used to complete his Mutual contract, could be rented from the Climax Company (director Mr Keller). Climax's representative, Mr Caulfield, had presented the brothers with a rental offer, but Jasper was under the impression that even if they did all the updates the studio needed, Climax had the right to sell the studio right out from under them. Or they could probably buy the property outright for $25,000 cash. He wrote to Syd that Charlie was not happy with the offer and wanted to consider building in San Diego, where he believed the city would pay the costs of construction. Another option was to simply choose another spot to build in Los Angeles, which, obviously, was the choice they finally made.[22] The approximately five-acre plot at the corner of La Brea, Sunset, and De Longpre in Hollywood, the former R.S. McClellan property, had been purchased as the appropriate spot for the new studio. It contained a largish Victorian house, which Syd would use for a while, and a bunch of old orange trees, with 600ft of frontage on La Brea, 300 on De Longpre and 300 on Sunset. The front of the studios proper would be on the La Brea side and would be six buildings 'arranged as to give the effect of a picturesque English village street. As planned, they offer no hint in their appearance of the purpose for which they are intended. The stages, dressing-rooms and other buildings will be well back from the street and out of the view of passers-by.'[23] The Milwaukee Building Company (Myer & Holler) were placed in charge of the planning and construction at a cost of approximately $100,000.

After this announcement in the papers on Tuesday 16 October, protests had been made to the City Council and rejected by that body by the end of that week, 18 or 19 October, in a vote of eight to one, the one being Councilman Conway. Protestants had claimed that its location would cause possible injury to residents in the vicinity (as it was in a residential neighborhood) and that it was too close to Hollywood High School, located at 1521 N. Highland Avenue, only a short three blocks away. This second was brought forward by the high school's principal, who urged the passage of an ordinance that would have affected seven of the major film companies in the area. If passed, it would have disallowed any film studio or allied operation within 1,000ft of an educational institution, thereby effecting Lasky, Fox, Metro, Peralta, Rolin, Horsley, Ince, as well as the Chaplin studios.[24] After taking the Council members on a tour of the property, Syd Chaplin and Jasper Johns were able to convince most of them that both concerns were without merit.[25] In addition, a contingent from the Merchant and Manufacturers Association presented a compelling argument against the ordinance:

> No other industry has contributed so much to the welfare of this community as the film studios, that spend millions of dollars each year in improvements, payrolls, and merchandise in almost every line. It is a well-known fact among the merchants that had it not been for the maintenance and expenditures of the motion-picture industry, the business of this community would have been seriously affected.[26]

A contingent of real estate developers from San Diego standing by ready to make the film folks one or two flattering offers to relocate probably helped the Los Angeles Councilmen to decide quickly in Chaplin's favor.

Actual work on the buildings began the week of 19 November, as reported in the press, because that was when the permits came in.

One report noted that Charlie took a shovel, Syd a pickaxe and the two preceded to remove some earth from the property before a few witnesses, soon allowing the actual workmen to get started:

> There were no speeches, fireworks or brass bands. Everything was done in a very quiet manner, without a barbecue and usual handshaking. A few of the nearby neighbors knew something was happening, but the community as a whole was ignorant of the proceedings.[27]

Included in the list of approved buildings were a large laboratory, an administration building, a scene dock, a property-room building, and a large steel-and-glass cage.[28] The Chaplin brothers marked the start of construction, as Robinson notes, with a brief film that included the two hoisting the first shovelfuls of dirt. Later additions to the film include Eric Campbell dressed as a magician introducing what seem to be the studio buildings appearing out of thin air in puffs of smoke and other such camera tricks. Unfortunately, Campbell, a stalwart member of Chaplin's Mutual troupe of players (the heavy) would not experience life under the First National contract, for he died in a car crash on 20 December 1917. The studio his magician made appear, however, still lives on to this day – beyond the lives of all of its players.

Chaplin and company moved in after the New Year's holiday in January 1918, the industry press having reported on 20 December that the construction was nearing completion: 'the foundations for the last group of buildings were laid this week and, simultaneously with this, work was started on the erection of the steel structure for the glass studio.'[29] Work was to be completed within three weeks. Yet, it was important to portray a semblance of being in business in the new year. John Jasper, the manager of the Lone Star studio that Chaplin utilized during the Mutual period stayed on, but his tenure was to be short. Jasper had only been with Chaplin since May 1917, as indicated in a letter to him from Mutual Films' John Freuler, but he seems to have proven himself to both Charlie and Sydney during that time. Other company players who remained were Edna Purviance, Loyal Underwood, Henry Bergman, Albert Austin, Tom Wilson, and Jack Wilson, who would assist lead cameraman Rollie Totheroh behind the camera. Chaplin was bound by his new contract to always have three cameras in operation during shooting. Other studios staff included Carlyle Robinson, publicity director, Melville Brown and Charles Lapworth, members of Chaplin's personal staff (Chuck Riesner would join this group later), Danny Hall, technical director and Frank Crompton, director of construction.[30]

The first two orders of business involved new personnel. Chaplin's old Karno boss, Alf Reeves arrived at the Chaplin studios on 15 January to take up the position of stage manager. He was in ill health, thanks to his war service, and needed the warmth and healing effects of the California sunshine to ease him back into good condition. Syd arranged the job and Alf and his wife Amy showed up and stayed for the rest of their lives. But Alf was not to be relegated to stage manager for long.

The second addition to the Chaplin studios personnel was Chuck Riesner or C. Francis Riesner as he's labeled in the press. He came to the Chaplin studios as a well-seasoned vaudeville performer and entered Chaplin's employ on 16 January 1918.[31] While not as big as Eric Campbell, with his particular 'mug' he could certainly play the heavy, which he was to do in several First National Films, but also proved useful in writing gags and 'co-directing.' He became the third in Chaplin's personal triumvirate of assistants, along with Charles Lapworth and Melville Brown. Riesner was important to the careers of both Chaplin brothers in that he was the only director that could deal with Syd over the course of his five-picture Warner Brothers contract in the 1920s, only dropping out of the last one in exasperation. He seemed to realize what he had to do to keep himself in the good graces of each Chaplin to get what he himself wanted and needed. For the most part, he succeeded in doing just that.

By 20 January, Chaplin was ready to let in the press, namely the *Los Angeles Times*'s Grace Kingsley, and she brought the illustrator Gale along with her. Chaplin had already begun work on his initial First National effort, which was to be titled *A Dog's Life*, but came round to lead the two on a brief tour during a break, commenting:

> I think I could like this place if I didn't work here ... See, here's a lemon orchard back of the stage. Think lemons must be my lucky fruit – can't escape 'em – had a lemon orchard back of us at Essanay and one at the Lone Star – hope they keep the lemons in the orchard, though ... No, I'm not going to live in the studio – Brother Sid and Mrs Sid are going to try it, but none of the put-out-the-dog-and-let-in-the-cat-and-lock-the-cellar-door-stuff for me at my workshop ... But, see I've got a beautiful apartment – it's a large corner room, where there are bay windows and odd little dormer windows – this is to be a combination office and reception-room, and there's a door I can dodge out of and climb a tree in the lemon orchard if I want to get away from anybody ... Yes, there's a nice big swimming pool and there's a tennis court, both to be used for business and pleasure.[32]

A similarly dated article by *Pictures and the Picturegoer*'s Elsie Codd noted also that Chaplin intended to invest about half a million in the studio complex, although various reports placed this sum about a quarter of a million higher or lower. She described the innovations Chaplin hoped to apply to the main stage, basically a new light diffusing system that would allow dispensing with the old glass coverings used in the past, while allowing for particular Pacific climactic conditions that might arise.[33] By the time both of these lady reporters had presented their readers with their own impressions of the magnificent Chaplin Studios, its production reports had well begun, its first production tentatively titled *I Should Worry*, having shot 405ft of film on that auspicious first day.[34] Chaplin started the New Year with a party to end all parties, a banquet at the Alexandria Hotel in downtown Los Angeles. Ten of Chaplin's closest friends and family, all men, were invited, including Chuck Riesner, Charles Lapworth, Albert Austin, Carlyle R. Robinson, John Jasper, Melville Brown, Rollie Totheroh, Frank Crompton, and Henry Bergman.[35]

Chapter 2

First Film *A Dog's Life* (1918) and the Third Liberty Loan Tour

I n his first brilliant short film for First National, later to be titled *A Dog's Life*, Chaplin juxtaposed the life of the Little Tramp with the life of a street dog, 'Scraps,' correlating their daily experiences frame for frame almost, thereby demonstrating just how much alike all living things in similar situations really are. Scraps was Chaplin's first of many sidekicks, all successful, especially considering what a solitary character the Little Tramp really was. According to one account, Chaplin had muddled over many possible plot ideas during his long four-month holiday and settled on the idea of placing the Little Tramp out in the elements to try his luck and see what he got up to, adding the dog in like circumstances later. Music hall star Harry Lauder, during his visit to the studios, happened to refer to Chaplin's life as 'a dog's life' and the remark became the film's title. The film begins with the Little Tramp sleeping out in the open and soon being awakened by the fragrance of a hot-dog vendor moving through the landscape nearby, giving him an opportunity for a klepped breakfast of sorts, one a passing cop puts the kibosh on.

Chaplin's company of actors only changed slightly for this film. Edna Purviance continued as Chaplin's leading lady. While some scenes required many extras, if the avid Chaplin fan looked closely, he or she could see that many faces looked familiar, even if they might not have big parts: James T. Kelley, Henry Bergman (usually in drag), Loyal Underwood, Albert Austin, John Rand and even Syd's wife Minnie Chaplin acted as a burlesque dancer[1] in the Green Lantern.

Hearing-impaired landscape painter Granville Redmond[2] came on board as the proprietor of the Green Lantern; brother Syd took a turn as the lunch cart operator, [3] in a very fine example of classic comic timing, and Chuck Riesner acted as the employment office clerk. And, of course, there was Scraps and his fellow dog-pound denizens, many of whom were rented for a dollar a day.

Of course, as with films today, scenes were not shot chronologically. According to the studio production reports, the first scene shot was the employment office scene, featuring the Little Tramp, some recognizable regulars like Henry Bergman, Loyal Underwood, James T. Kelly and Albert Austin, but including a few other extra men too. Chaplin rehearsed with Tom Wilson in costume as the cop on the 22 January in the initial street scene mentioned above however, then production halted on the 23 January when Harry Lauder stopped by the studios for a visit. According to the production reports, using two cameras, 745ft of film were shot of the two men clowning for the cameras, to be used to help the war effort, part of which consisted of them swapping their totemic elements of costuming, with Chaplin donning the tam, the intricate cane and the pipe, and Lauder the bowler, the cane, and the cigarette. Lauder had dropped by to try to collect some funds for his British Wounded Soldiers Fund, a $1,000 check for which Chaplin can be seen handing to Lauder at the end of their one-reeler. The short film was to have garnered the cause millions more than that if it had been shown throughout Europe (save Germany, of course) but, in fact, it was never shown. [4]

Visitors and other diversions kept shooting from being very productive until the 28th, but that day, despite an attempt to stage a dog fight, not much successful film was shot. Dog scenes were also shot on 30 and 31 January and 3 and 4 February. These scenes correlated with the initial scenes of the Little Tramp 'sparring' with the cop to obtain the hot-dog surreptitiously; Scraps, meanwhile, was fighting the other mongrels for a bone. By 5 February, Chaplin had reverted his attention to the hot dog wagon and was rehearsing that scene, which he was then shooting on 6 February; by 9 February, he was changing the story and took the day off to work on new gags. Interestingly, there was now no title on the production reports for the project, either. The report for 11 February stated that it marked the beginning of a new story, but that everything shot to that point would be used in the new story. It may have been at this point that since the two spies were unveiled the week before, much of the written and decided-upon gags had to be revised. The press reported that during the time when the Chaplin studios had opened its doors to the public (all a person needed was a card of introduction to be admitted, and some 2,500 people were), two enterprising young people, a man and a woman claiming to be journalists, were caught standing outside Chaplin's bungalow one day while a brainstorming session was taking place. Chaplin calmly asked them to enter and once inside, they were frisked and relieved of their belongings, which entailed the following:

1. Eight sketches of completed sets.
2. Books containing stenographic notes explaining every detail during action.
3. Minute descriptions of the characters surrounding Charlie, and a careful record of every costume used.

The newspaper they claimed to work for and even their names and addresses were all fictitious. The result of this fiasco was that much of the story had to be reworked and gags had to be rewritten. From that day forward, no guests were allowed on the studio grounds during filming and guards were posted at the entrances to make sure of this.[5] Details of the plots of Chaplin films would be kept from the media until a week before each film's release as well. Difficult lesson learned.

So, the film's title changed to *Wiggle and Son*, but only for one day. The report for 12 February stated that the title had returned to *I Should Worry* because more footage was being shot for that film project, some 516ft, so clearly some distinction was being made between the two projects at this point, or this demarcated the point at which the rewriting had to occur, due to the security breach. The next several days denote interruptions for visitors and for writing gags, so not much filming took place, but the title remained *I Should Worry*. On 18 February, filming was delayed due to the prop pocketbook being misplaced. On 26 February, Syd received a letter in response to one of his to J.D. Williams, one of the First National managers, which hints that the letter Syd had sent to Williams had tried to assuage him in regard to why the first film was taking so long to finish. Williams remarked that he was very glad to receive the letter and was 'surely glad to hear that the first picture is progressing nicely. I think he is quite right in taking his time and assuring himself of turning out a production that will be better than any heretofore made by him, as a great deal depends upon his first picture.'[6]

By 7 March, Chaplin was shooting bar scenes in which he enters the bar with the dog's wagging tail visible hanging out the back of his clothing. As an unattributed *Dallas* (Texas) *Times Herald* reporter described:

the dance hall of the character for which Coney Island, the bowery and the tenderloin of Chicago were famous some twenty years ago, where the 'celebrities' of the underworld gave and took fractured skulls as nightly souvenirs, is the featured scene [in this initial First National effort].

[…]

The incomparable Charles has turned himself loose among an aggregation of desperadoes that would have made the notorious Jesse James gang turn green with envy. And he goes in single-handed, without gun or knife, trusting his safety to his own cleverness and what little protection might be influenced through the presence of his dog.[7]

One hundred people were used in the scene to enhance this sense of authenticity. By 9 March, it was reported that Chaplin would be stomping for Liberty Loan bonds in the southern states on the Third Liberty Loan tour beginning in April, so behind the scenes he was still working to deflect whatever bad press the war was causing him.[8]

The report for 23 March stated that filming had completed the day before and cutting had begun on *A Dog's Life*, the first time this title was used or mentioned. Retakes were completed on 25 March and all hands assisted in editing the film beginning on 26 March. Chaplin left for the Third Liberty Loan Tour on 1 April and his colleagues back at the studio were still cutting the film, finishing at last on 5 April. Only on this date was it announced that the film would be a three-reeler, rather than the expected two-reeler, causing some chaos among theater owners.[9] Syd then left immediately for Chicago to turn the negative over to the 'patiently' waiting First National bosses.[10] When he arrived at the Rothacker Plant,[11] the company charged with making the prints, he was welcomed by Tally who traded the two negatives for a $140,000 check and so the process of creating the prints began.[12] Also kept under wraps was the plot of the Chaplin film, except for the fact that it involved a dog in some manner. So, all that was leaked about the film's story upon its completion was that as the film opens, the Little Tramp,

was aroused from profound slumber in a fence-corner by the aroma from the wares of a passing hot dog vendor until his final triumph over a gang of cabaret crooks to a resort to which he and the dog have wandered on the trail of a beautiful, innocent-eyed young singer, there [being] no occasion when the action does not make full demands upon Charlie's powers of expression.[13]

The *Moving Picture World* writing office, however, were given an early screening of the film on 14 April, their reviews then being printed in the 27 April edition of the journal. One writer, 'G.B.', seemed to especially get at what it was that Chaplin achieved so well:

> In *A Dog's Life*, we see not a new Chaplin. We see one ripened and broadened. His long holiday has brightened a wit always on keen edge, as illustrated by the newfangled chase around and under the fence … Most laughable is the comedy, and consequently all the greater is the reaction in the periods where pathos dominates.[14]

By 4 May, it was being announced in the press that the response to Chaplin's first effort for First National was overwhelming:

> The showing of 'A Dog's Life' first of Charlie Chaplin's comedies, in all houses operating under First National franchises during the week of April 14 resulted in unprecedented business. Attendance records have been broken in many of the largest theaters in America, and it would not be surprising if the First National stockholders get back on this single release most of the money they have invested in the entire series.[15]

By 1 June, Tally announced that he was extending the run of *A Dog's Life* for the fourth week in his houses. After having made an initial decision to end the run after a fortnight, he found that box office receipts were 'steadily increasing as the word-of-mouth advertising of enthusiastic fans began to get in its effect, so he extended the run.'[16] Even the death of Mutt, AKA Scraps, Chaplin's co-star, a short month after the film wrapped, received quite a bit of coverage in the press, especially due to his fatal malady, which was deemed 'a broken heart,' due to the fact that Chaplin was away from the studio on the Liberty Bond tour.[17] In August, Tally came by the studio to present Chaplin with a commemorative *A Dog's Life Book*, which was a leather-bound volume with gilded lettering on the cover and which contained inside 'copies of advanced advertising, colored plates, autographed letters from members of the circuit who ran the picture, and a large number of criticisms and clippings,'[18] but most unusual was the title page, which featured a portrait of Tally at the top, that was encircled by portraits of the other First National exhibitors all around the page (including Syd and Charlie Chaplin) and the words in the center in Gothic script:

To T.L. Tally, Vice President, First National Exhibitors, Incorporated, in dedicating to you this address, your co-directors and fellow members of the First National Exhibitors Circuit desire to record the capability with which you have acted in your Vice Presidential capacity to this Circuit and to express their admiration at your success in signing the world's greatest comedy picture star Charles Chaplin for this organization.[19]

This clearly indicated that the album had not been made for Chaplin at all, but for Tally himself, yet Tally pawned it off to the press as a generous big deal on his part anyway, perhaps providing a bit of information about his true nature with the act.

With all this publicity, it is a shame First National did not keep the idea that they had already recouped their money on the first film in mind, because dark days were ahead. In any event, both Chaplin and Company and the First National brass could not have been more pleased with the result of this first effort and so they spent the time that Chaplin was away selling Liberty bonds formulating their own response to Chaplin's critics, submitting the following to the press during this period:

Mr Chaplin's pictures are giving the soldiers in the trenches the greatest relaxation they could find. In addition to that, he is buying war stocks heavily. Mr Chaplin has a perfect right to resent being termed, in any sense, a 'slacker.' He is doing a thousand times more good for the world by doing what he is than if he were in the trenches. People fail to realize that at this depressing time, the man who can make them smile and forget the terrible, worldwide gloom is doing a real good for humanity.

The bright and shiny four-year-old Federal Reserve and its leader, Treasury Secretary William Gibbs McAdoo, came up with the idea shortly after America entered the war in late April 1917 that its public must finance the war in some manner. Taxation (raising taxes) would only afford so much, so some other method must be put into action and that method would be war bonds. McAdoo pitched the plan to the public as their patriotic duty, making interest rates on the bonds lower than banks were offering so that wealthy individuals and companies would not snap them up and that some effort by volunteers would be needed to sell them. Bonds started at $50 and ended at $10,000, providing bond pricing within almost everyone's reach. The plan eventually fell into four organized drives over two years, two in 1917 and two in 1918.[20] Hollywood stars and other celebrities were enlisted to tour the country and sell bonds, with the totals of their efforts hitting the press and adding in some measure to their personal caché. Chaplin is noted to have subscribed $100,000 in the First Liberty Loan drive,[21] but this was without touring or hawking the bonds to others. As mentioned in Chapter 1, he would be pushed further into the campaign in October 1917, when he agreed to give a pro-Liberty Bond speechlet in Hilo, Hawaii. By March 1918, his initial First National film nearly completed, he would have been much more easily persuaded to join the Third Liberty Loan tour for a longer commitment. After all, his friends Doug and Mary were on board. And he needed to work out what sort of film he would produce next anyway.

Douglas Fairbanks, Mary Pickford, and Chaplin took the train east together on 1 April, with the idea that they would triple-up their energies in Liberty bond sales in Chicago, Washington, D.C., Philadelphia, and New York City before splitting off and attacking sections of the country individually. Salt Lake City, Utah, was the first short stop on 2 April and crowds waiting there braved a late spring blizzard for hours to see their film favorites, necessitating the services of the marines, the police, and soldiers to break a pathway through them to the speaking platform.[22] Fairbanks was the only one of the three with energy enough to engage the crowds at the station there initially:

> As the train pulled into the depot there rose such a shout that the walls of the structure trembled and even the shrill shriek of the engines could not be heard in the din.
>
> Boys yelled and jumped, women screamed, men shouted, and the guards and police were overpowered by nearly 20,000 people when it was realized that the famous trio had arrived. They burst through the gates and swarmed upon the train crying out for Doug, Mary and Charley. Only Fairbanks dared to brave the multitude that surrounded the train. He made a flying leap from the train right into the crowds and followed the band that led the way to the speaking platform, which was erected in the depot. [23]

Eventually, Pickford and Chaplin briefly joined Fairbanks on the stage.

The next stop was Omaha, Nebraska, where the trio stopped at 10.00 pm on 3 April. Fairbanks took center stage again, making a short speech from an observation car, but this time both Pickford and Chaplin were with him. Pickford stole the show in her bright peacock blue brocade coat. Chaplin only tipped his derby to the crowd and helped Pickford's mother into her place before them. The stop lasted just one half-hour. [24]

The plan for Chicago was for the three to arrive on 4 April in time for luncheon at the Auditorium hotel, at which approximately 150 Chicago businessmen, members of the Paramount staff and exhibitors would join them in the Gold Room. Afterwards, there was to be a parade up Michigan Avenue led by Chaplin in costume.[25] This was the pie-in-the-sky version. What really happened was that the three landed at the station, refused interviews, then gave in, went to the Blackstone Hotel for an informal reception, had luncheon, drove around the city, and left on another train for Washington, D.C. at 5.30 pm.[26] One more stop was made, however, before they reached the capital, and that was in Harrisburg, Pennsylvania. The train was late, but the huge crowd waited anyway, even hanging onto the fenders of the three cars that took Chaplin and Fairbanks to the city square for the formalities (Pickford sat this one out). Schools let out and many offices closed, all to see the two stars before them for a total of twenty minutes.[27]

Washington, D.C. on 6 April was to be the official kick-off of the Third Liberty Loan campaign, the main part of which was to be held in the forecourt of the State, War and Navy building near 17th Street and State Place. When the Big Three arrived, they were joined by actress Marie Dressler and Franklin D. Roosevelt, then Assistant Secretary of the Navy, to whom Fairbanks sold his first Liberty bond on the spot. Thousands of people were in attendance for the event. The celebrities led a parade down Pennsylvania Avenue via horse-drawn carriage to the designated platform where the speeches began in earnest, Chaplin becoming so overwhelmed at one point that he fell off the stage taking Dressler with him, both then landing squarely upon FDR. It seemed all part of the act.[28] By the end of the day, Chaplin, Fairbanks, and Dressler had each sold $100,000 worth of bonds, with Pickford topping that with her total of $1.6 million worth.[29]

Really, the Third Liberty Loan was the only drive to which Chaplin gave any quantifiable energy, whereas Fairbanks, in one example, was heavily involved in all four. This is easily explained by two transparent facts: 1) Chaplin was not a U.S. citizen, even though he was trying to appear patriotic, and 2) he had a new film contract that he very much needed to attend to. Clearly, he gained a lot of energy from his friend Fairbanks, too, which can be seen in photographs and films of the rallies in Washington, D.C. and on Wall Street in New York City, the next stop. Once Fairbanks and Chaplin went their own ways, however, Chaplin's energy for the task quickly diminished.

Noon of Monday, 8 April, was perhaps the icing on the cake of this joint send-off for the Third Liberty Loan, for Fairbanks and Chaplin staged a rally at the corner of Broad and Wall streets in the Financial District at the foot of the bronze George Washington statute outside the Sub-Treasury building surrounded by what was then the largest-ever crowd to attend such an event – about 20,000 people. Photos show the two small figures of Fairbanks and Chaplin seemingly awash in this crowd of thousands of be-hatted and be-suited gentlemen, all losing their comportment in response to Fairbanks's acrobatics and Chaplin's comic leading of a 'khaki-clad' band:

> Not only was the asphalt paved solidly from building line to building line in four directions as far as the eye could see, but also there were walls of humanity reaching to the zenith as the walls of the Bankers Trust Building and the other towering office buildings flew up. Clerks and stenographers and offices boys, yes, and bosses, too, leaned far out the windows up near the clouds to get a glimpse of the tops of the heads of George and Charley and Doug.[30]

Chaplin had appeared first and gave what he told the crowd was his first speech:

> Human life is at stake and no one ought to worry about what rate of interest the bonds are going to bring or what he can make by purchasing them. Money is needed, money to support the great army and navy of Uncle Sam. This very minute the Germans occupy a position of advantage, and we have got to get the dollars. It ought to go over so that we can drive that old devil, the Kaiser,

out of France. How many of you men, how many of you boys out there, have bought or are willing to buy Liberty bonds?[31]

After some hijinks at the Sub-Treasury Building where the two were privileged to hold $100 million cash in their hot little hands for a few moments, Chaplin and Fairbanks departed New York the next morning to meet up with Pickford in Philadelphia for a final joint meeting before their dispersal onto individual routes. Pickford, her mother, and publicity director arrived first around 11.00 am, followed closely by Chaplin, Fairbanks, and their two publicity directors in another train, joining select members of the Liberty Loan drive of Philadelphia on a rainy blustery day in the city. After a few words from the stars, the parties left the station, stopping first at the Liberty statue in front of City Hall, then making their way to the Bellevue Stratford Hotel. Chaplin, Pickford, and Fairbanks were allowed to rest until the 1.30 pm luncheon, because the inclement weather had forced the cancelation of all other outdoor activities planned for that morning. After luncheon, the party was walked a block down to the Academy of Music where the 3.30 pm rally was to be held and at which each of the stars gave a short speech promoting the sale of the bonds.[32] They were given dinner at the home of Mrs E.T. Stotesbury at 6.30 pm and then taken to the Second Regiment Armory at 8.30 pm for a mass meeting and a second round of speeches.[33] Thus ended their collaborative efforts for the Third Liberty Loan.

Chaplin's first individual event would be in the town of Petersburg, Virginia on 11 April. He had been relying only on his publicity agent, Carlyle Robinson, who had been with him since the beginning of the tour, and most likely his valet Tom Harrington, but now he added a few others: one of the three personal assistants who worked for him at the Chaplin studios, Charles Lapworth, and his friend Rob Wagner, who had joined him on his recent trip to Hawaii back in October 1917. Lapworth's affiliation with the Chaplin Studios and with Chaplin was probably a strategic move on Chaplin's part.

Lapworth was a former employee of Lord Northcliffe in that he wrote for the *Daily Mail* in London. The fact that Chaplin snapped him up when he had the opportunity, adding him to his staff as one of three personal assistants, is probably no accident. Who would be more able to help Chaplin navigate the waters of Northcliffe's ire than a former employee? And Lapworth himself certainly didn't suffer under the bargain, becoming Samuel Goldwyn's European representative, then the manager of Gainsborough Pictures in Britain and on up the ladder. That his time with Chaplin was not either negative or detrimental is evidenced by a letter he wrote to Chaplin well after he had left the studio, dated 14 February 1919:

> Have many recollections of our month's trip, not the least amusing of which was the episode where the 400 young ladies in white got up and sang their song of welcome, when I filed into the great hall following the Chairman. They thought that I was the great man, and for two full glorious minutes I realized what greatness was. Of course, the 400 young ladies were stung. You didn't appear until 9.00 pm and then they had not the courage to admit their previous mistake by singing their song to you. But, under the rose, your sensitive musical ear was thereby saved from pain the most excruciating.[34]

Wagner, a progressive and a socialist, was on the FBI's radar and, unfortunately for Chaplin, brought that misery along with him on the tour. Archival documents at the University of California, Los Angeles, Library Special Collections show that the FBI started following him (and 'Chaplin Party,' including Lapworth, Murphy, Harrington, Chaplin and Wagner) from venue to venue on this trip. Wagner was of interest to the FBI, because he was believed to have troubling pro-German affiliations. The aforementioned 'Murphy,' was one John R. Murphy, an FBI agent working undercover within the Chaplin party itself. C.L. Keep wrote on 25 April 1918, that a memorandum book had been taken surreptitiously from Wagner at the Grunewald Hotel in New Orleans. The contents were then dictated into a Dictaphone and had yet to be returned to Wagner without his notice. Unfortunately for the Bureau, Wagner had already started his return to Los Angeles with Tom Harrington, Chaplin's valet. Only the remaining Chaplin party members (including the spy) traveled onto Washington, D.C., where concluding Loan tour activities were to be held.[35]

In Petersburg, Chaplin was greeted once again by a heavy spring snowstorm, which failed to deter his audience at the Academy of Music where the festivities were held. Chaplin's speech garnered subscriptions of $350,000 in bonds by the close of the morning, in what appeared to be a successful first solo appearance.[36] He was on to Richmond, Virginia, for an additional meeting at the City Auditorium there beginning at 7.45 pm. The John Marshall High School chorus and Kessnick's band provided some musical entertainment before the speeches began. Chaplin entered the auditorium at full throttle, jumping on a table and leading some 4,000 people in the audience in a rendition of *Over There*, then began collecting subscription cards himself, nearly causing a stampede. At this point, he got the idea to start selling his stunts for largish bond sales – $5,000 for a pratfall, another nice sum for the roll of his derby down his arm and yet another sum for the silly walk. As for the war and the sacrifice young American soldiers were making, Chaplin remarked:

> Never mind how serious it is. We're going to win – we've got to win – the sooner it's over, the better and that depends on cooperation. This is the Third Liberty Loan. Let's over-subscribe it, so we won't have to have a fourth. Never mind doubling it, triple it, quadruple it![37]

Chaplin's personal assistant, Charles Lapworth, also gave a short speech. Chaplin was on the road again at 9.40 pm for Raleigh, where he was to speak the next day.[38]

But Raleigh was two cities down the line. The next stop was actually Rocky Mount, North Carolina, where Chaplin was to stop the morning of Friday, 12 April. He was scheduled to arrive there at 10.30 am, which he did, touring the small town and then joining a patriotic parade at 1.00 pm, the likes of which had never been seen there. It included Boy Scouts, Girl Scouts, labor organizations, the Red Cross, hundreds of automobiles, and the State College band of Raleigh. Chaplin then spoke at 2.00 pm at the Farmer's Mutual warehouse. He spoke energetically for over an hour and was followed by short speeches made by others in his party, leaving shortly thereafter for Wilson.[39] Arriving by train at 3.30 pm on a snowy, sleety day, and an impromptu procession to the Banner tobacco warehouse was formed involving:

A. and E. brass band, Uncle Sam float, Kaiser float, Women's Club, United Daughters of the Confederacy, Chamber of Commerce, Rotary Club, Merchants' Association, Tobacco Board of Trade and float, Camp fire girls, home guards, Atlantic Christian college students and hundreds of children from the graded schools [from surrounding counties.][40]

After being introduced, Chaplin spoke briefly, followed by Charles Lapworth.

Only after those two engagements did he finally arrive in Raleigh, scheduled for 4.05 pm, but arriving much later and having to miss entertaining folks in the street. Raleigh being Carlyle Robinson's hometown, it was mentioned in the press that he was especially looking forward to experiencing some nice festivities there.[41] The event was booked at the city auditorium, which held a revival every Friday night, so the Liberty Loan event was scheduled to follow hard on that event. Essentially, the revival would be broken up as soon as Chaplin arrived. But the revival and its leader, Dr. L.R. Scarborough effortlessly transformed their meeting into an energetic patriotic rally for the Liberty Loaners and the attendance quickly ballooned to 5,000. Chaplin's party had now fleshed out to the aforementioned group in the discussion of Rob Wagner, probably because Wagner was now aboard. In fact, James R. Murphy, the FBI plant, who was supposed to keep an eye on Wagner, gave a serious anti-German speech that night, mentioning, for instance, that both the wool industry and the tobacco industry had, before the war started, been almost exclusively in German hands. Charles Lapworth followed with a short speech and then Chaplin was introduced, choosing to make no speech, but instead to entertain, wildly gesticulating to the crowd and whipping them into a frenzy. He was asked to walk comically across the stage when a certain sales total was reached, at which time he 'flopped, sidled, skidded and stumbled.'[42] It being kiddies' night, too, Chaplin greeted each child that brought a subscription up to the stage. The end-of-night total was $92,000, but someone chipped in another $8,000 to make it an even $100,000 for reputation's sake.

Saturday 13 April, the Chaplin party arrived in Greensboro, North Carolina. Earlier that week, the *Daily News* published an article asking readers to take carloads of school children from High Point, North Carolina (and, most likely, other small towns in the vicinity) to be part of the Liberty Loan parade which was to take place Saturday morning at 10.30 am to greet Chaplin and his party.[43] Overall, Greensboro, or at least the reporter writing for its *Daily News*, seemed less impressed with Chaplin than with the event his fellow citizens had put on. Chaplin and his party took part in the biggest parade ever seen in the city, launched for the event; he made a few remarks at the State Normal College, attended the luncheon with the Rotarians at the Smith Memorial building, but few specifics of his visit beyond that were related.[44] At 2.00 pm he was greeting folks in Winston-Salem as he was driven in via motorcar. Chaplin had managed to acquire a cold the day before and needed to rest at a hotel for a few hours before he met the masses in this city. Even when the show opened at the Auditorium, Charles Lapworth started the speeches, alerting the audience, too, that Chaplin was under the weather. Still, when Chaplin came on, he gave the audience his usual serious talk, but ended on a light note: 'For a $5,000 subscription, I will kiss the subscriber, and ... for a $10,000 one, I will marry her!'[45] Perhaps the most poignant moment of this visit was when Chaplin was asked to stop his car on the way out of town to visit little Fred O'Brien, sick and in a wheelchair. He not only had the car stop but went inside the house to greet the boy. Perhaps one of the most interesting points to come out of this effort on Chaplin's part is the strength of character it shows in him. The day-in and day-out grueling schedule of two or three stops packed with social activities and speeches – it just seems so out of character for Chaplin in every way.

Lexington, North Carolina then was the next stop; Chaplin arrived early enough to have a short nap at the March Hotel, before being taken over to the courthouse to the speaker's platform there. Charles Lapworth again spoke first, but Chaplin spoke seriously for about fifteen minutes, making a good impression on the locals.[46] The trick was for the citizens to sign their checks for the bonds to Chaplin, then he would endorse them to the Treasury department, so that when the buyer received his or her check back, Chaplin's signature would be on it as a nifty keepsake of the event. So, he spent time signing those until it was time to take the train on to Salisbury, the next town on the tour.

The first thing on the agenda at Salisbury was dinner at the Empire Hotel. Afterwards the party was driven to the tabernacle about two blocks away for the evening's festivities. Mayor Woodson started off by reading a telegram from Raleigh stating that although only $92,000 had been raised during the rally in Raleigh, the total had risen to $100,000 before midnight that night, so would Mr Chaplin please stand on his head for the Salisbury audience as he promised in Raleigh? Chaplin replied 'By heck, I'll do it.' and went down backwards before rolling up on his head and sticking his feet straight up.[47] After this glorious performance, which made the papers far beyond the deep South, Chaplin and party were on their way to Charlotte, North Carolina, where they were to spend the night and appear the next day in two different venues, actually three if Camp Greene military training camp just outside of town is to be counted.

After a restful night, the Chaplin party motored out to Camp Greene about 12.30 pm. The group was organized by local personality Clarence O. Kuester, who brought along some additional friends, all of whom met at camp headquarters and were then ushered around the camp by Major Hines. The caravan of cars moved slowly through the camp,

> past a crowd of soldiers loitering about, and one lad would happen to recognize Charlie as the man who has made millions laugh. A shout would put his companions wise and before the machine, in which Charlie rode, had gone 50 feet further, it would be brought to a stop. For the soldier boys were swarming about it, urging Charlie 'ole boy' to get out and pay them a visit. And Charlie did.[48]

Eventually, they reached the headquarters of the 59th Infantry and were invited into mess by Colonel Atkinson, later posing for pictures with the young soldiers, one of whom included Chaplin holding a soldier's mess kit filled with dollar bills, a silent indication of the money needed to feed an army at war. He even graced the boys with his funny walk at one point, something he was rarely doing on the tour, since he was keeping to a more serious persona given the gravity of his mission.

Back in Charlotte, Chaplin had two more events scheduled for later in the day there. The first event was held at the City Auditorium at 2.30 pm (actual time 3.05 pm) and followed what had now become a familiar organizational structure for Chaplin, with Charles Lapworth speaking first, acting as a sort of warm-up for him, followed by Chaplin appearing from behind a curtain announcing 'Howdy-do!' to whatever city he happened to be in. He spoke for ten minutes, led some cheers for the army and navy, then persuaded Director Hawley of the 77th Field Artillery Band to allow him to take over, leading the musicians more confidently than any of them would have ever imagined. Within an hour the show was over, and Chaplin's party was transported to the next venue, the Old Presbyterian College. Although this second meeting was arranged expressly for the children, even Chaplin noticed that they were outnumbered by the adults in the audience.[49] At 4.55 pm, the group started out for Columbia, South Carolina, where they would spend the night and speak the next day.

As had been the case for Charlotte, the first order of the day for Columbia was to visit the soldiers at nearby Camp Jackson, where Chaplin was scheduled to speak at 11.00 am at the Liberty Theatre. Commanding officer of the camp, Major General Charles J. Bailey introduced Chaplin to an audience of some 4,000 soldiers. He graced them with one or two of his Charlie-esque tricks, then told them that he had nothing to say, because he could not, of course, ask them to buy Liberty bonds. But he did want to let them know that:

you are doing a grand thing, and the nation as a whole appreciates the service that you are rendering to her in this crisis. I cannot talk to you about war for you probably know more than I do about that subject, so the only thing that remains for me to do is to say, 'I am glad to see you.'[50]

With this, the boys broke into a rendition of *Hang the Kaiser on the Sour Apple Tree*, which Chaplin was able to join them in singing. After the program, he joined Major General Bailey at mess before the drive back to Columbia. He was driven down Main Street in Columbia from the Jefferson Hotel to the Columbia Theatre, where he was to speak at 1.30 pm. Because he didn't look like his familiar on-screen character, Chaplin was little recognized, especially when it was so advertised in the newspaper the day before.[51] However, he made up for it by throwing red roses to his admirers from the open back seat of the car. Chaplin gave his usual address to the theater audience, asked for his usual three cheers for the army and navy and was preceded on the podium by Charles Lapworth and local Columbian William D. Melton. Boy scouts passed out subscription blanks and once these were collected and Chaplin had endorsed them, the party made its way to the town of Sumter for another event about 4.40 pm.[52]

In Sumter, the Chaplin party staged the rally at a tobacco warehouse and may not have had much hope of landing many subscriptions, because the area had been 'well-combed' already, but 5,000 people showed up from the surrounding area and Chaplin was able to subscribe $17,000 worth of Liberty bonds – a very respectable amount. The lion's share of this amount was paid for, however, by Chaplin's usual challenge that a subscription of $5,000 would buy a headstand.[53] After Sumter, they returned to Columbia and spent the night.

The next day was Tuesday, 16 April, Chaplin's 29th birthday, and it would be auspicious for several reasons. All the newspapers seemed to be carrying the story that the local exemption board in Los Angeles had indeed called him up for service. Although the press seemed to know this, Chaplin himself had not yet received any documentation. Yet, what a great headline to greet a person on his birthday! Augusta did its best to make the day a happy one for Chaplin anyway. The Chaplin party arrived at Union Station at 1.45 pm, leaving shortly thereafter to visit soldiers at the Camp Hancock Hospital nearby. They were able to rest and freshen up at the Albion Hotel before taking the stage in the afternoon at the Wells Theatre on Broad Street (later renamed the Imperial Theatre and famously known by that name for many years). After the usual speeches and antics (Chaplin again successfully took the baton, this time directing the 110th Infantry Band from Camp Hancock), Chaplin and his party were treated to a special birthday dinner at the Augusta Country Club on Milledge

Road, hosted by Richmond County Superior Court Judge Henry Hammond.[54]

On 17 April, Chaplin's party performed at an event held at the Grand Theatre in Macon, Georgia, where thousands of people crowded in at noon to see the great comedian. The Chaplin party had arrived in Macon at 3.00 am from Augusta, were taken to the Dempsey Hotel and rose at 11.00 am in time to meet the Red Cross ladies on the 7th floor of the theater to tour their work room before the rally. Chaplin quite charmed the ladies, of course, and made 'a pretty little speech to them, in which he stated that the sight of so many women wearing "holy garments" inspired him to greater efforts for the task that he has undertaken.'[55] R.F. Burden, chair of the Bibb County Liberty Loan committee introduced J. Ellsworth Hall of Macon, who then introduced J.R. Murphy of the Chaplin party. Murphy spoke first before introducing Chaplin, who received a long ovation then led the audience in several cheers and was moved to lead the band, the 124th Infantry band, in a rendition of *Over There*. Skipping his usual ten-minute speech, he launched right into an appeal for subscriptions, listing the various amounts available. Whereas at other events, Chaplin had promised to stand on his head for a $5,000 subscription, the total this night was $100,000. The people of Macon, however, surpassed the total, so Chaplin performed the headstand graciously.[56]

The Chaplin party then arrived in Atlanta by train at 4.20 pm that afternoon.[57] Lapworth and Chaplin faced 8,000 adoring Atlantans that evening in the auditorium, garnering over $500,000 in subscriptions. Branford Knapp, head of the Extension Department of the Department of Agriculture spoke first, and despite his title, proved to be a rousing speaker. Then, after Lapworth's warm-up, Chaplin found himself in thrall to the huge crowd, doing tricks for subscriptions – silly walks, headstands, kissing pretty ladies, leading the band, leading the audience in heartfelt cheers for the military, and holding small children aloft before the audience. The crowd's enthusiasm for Chaplin and for subscribing in general required three stenographers, several counters, an adding machine expert and two full hours in the building. The reporter hastened to add that the majority of the subscriptions were 'of the masses,' being small denominations made by the men, women and children of the city.[58]

The next day, 18 April, received the most press coverage of the entire tour. The Chaplin party were supposed to roll into Nashville, Tennessee about 4.45 pm, but didn't make it until 6.10 pm, when they were escorted to the Hermitage Hotel by a welcoming party that included Mrs W.H. Lambeth. Children threw flowers at Chaplin's car as it drove by and a clerk from the Drifoos Hotel and Restaurant near the station gave Chaplin a custard pie, which he took along with him to the hotel. They were to attend a Kiwanis dinner at the Commercial Club, along with 400 businessmen and their wives, but this was also delayed. They asked Chaplin for a story when he finally arrived. At first, he begged off, because of the long train ride and feeling tired, but then he gave them this joke:

A young Irishman was captured by the Germans and was put in a German prison camp. Every time the German soldier who was on guard passed by the Irishman, he would call out, 'Wasn't that a terrible licking that the Irish gave the Germans at the Marne?' The German soldier became tired of hearing this and at last said to the Irishman, 'The next time that you say that you will be shot.' The Irishman made the statement again and was taken out to be shot but was given the choice of becoming a German subject or being shot. Thinking that a live German was better than a dead Irishman, he chose to be a German. The next time the Irishman saw his former German guard, he said, 'Say, Boche, that was a terrible licking we Germans got at the hands of the Irish, wasn't it?'[59]

Then it was on to the Ryman Auditorium for the main event at 8.30 pm. Dr. Miles Williams of the Kiwanis Club presided over the rally. Both J.R. Murphy and Charles Lapworth spoke, along with several others.[60] As had become a habit for these rallies, Chaplin led the band, this time in *Over There*, and when he wasn't happy with the audience's response, he made them do it all over. He then led them in the standard three cheers, did some stunts and motioned for the subscriptions to come forward. Subscriptions that night reached $375,000, bringing Nashville $150,000 over its quota.[61]

Given the energy required in Nashville, it's doubtful that the Chaplin party traveled all the way to Bowling Green, Kentucky, some 65.9 miles, for an event the next day as planned. The only evidence of this event is a document in the Chaplin archives, a sort of certificate to be given to subscribers that reads:

Certificate Chaplin Day, Bowling Green, Kentucky, April 19, 1918. This is to certify that [blank] has subscribed from me for [blank] dollars Liberty bonds of the Third Liberty Loan. I appreciate this as a practical example of patriotism. [followed by a blank line for Chaplin's signature].

The fact that this exists suggests that the event itself was canceled, because no similar documents were created for other events. Perhaps the certificates were given in lieu of an actual appearance if the citizens indeed chose to subscribe to the Liberty bond in Chaplin's name anyway. Nothing else, no other date or venue, seems to pop up as part of the agenda and there is no doubt that all members of the party needed a break by this point, so perhaps that is simply what happened – Bowling Green was canceled and they took the day off. They were due in Memphis the next day, a 212-mile trip, and starting from Bowling Green would have added on an additional sixty-six miles, another possible deciding factor, if they needed one. Paducah, Kentucky, too, was hoping for a visit from Chaplin in the coming week and published an article in their *Sun-Democrat* on 20 April that Chaplin had sent them a 'God Bless You' but would be unable to visit due to his declining health, no doubt brought on by the exhausting schedule.

Arriving in Memphis the morning of 20 April, Chaplin's health by this point obliged them to pare the day's program down to the bare minimum. Originally, the plan for Memphis looked like this:

> 1) a screening at 10.00 am of *My Four Years in Germany* followed by a speech at the Orpheum theater, 2) 3.00 pm at the Lyceum Theatre, 3) 4.00 pm at Overton Park, 4) 6.00 pm at Church's Park for the benefit of the negroes, 4) appearance at 8.00 pm at the Majestic No. 2, 5) appearance at 8.20 pm at the Princess Theatre, 6) appearance at 8.40 pm at the Orpheum Theatre, 7) appearance at 9.00 pm at the Majestic No. 1.[62]

There doesn't seem to be much empathy for the star or his compatriots interlaced into this original schedule anyway, and so they surely had no misgivings about canceling out on most of it. Chaplin did appear at Overton Park, explaining his over-worked condition and then also kept his appointment at Church's Park a bit later that evening. The cancelations of other events were announced in the paper that day, suggesting that his personal doctor had demanded the truncation of his schedule.

With the rally beginning at 6.00 pm at Overton Park, 5,000 Memphians braved the rainy and cold conditions to hear Chaplin speak, and, of course, were forced to hear a few other speakers first, including Murphy and Lapworth. As one reporter noted, however, it was clear why Chaplin 'was exhausted. Thousands of men, women and boys surged and pushed and nearly fought to get near him as he approached and left the platform in the midst of a police guard. Everyone wanted to shake his hand or pull his coat.'[63] This is more deeply emphasized by a sidebar in the paper entitled 'Crowd Mistook Metcalf for Charlie Chaplin,' which relates to the fact that the poor postmaster for Memphis, Charles Metcalf, reached the park in one of the two Chaplin cars before Chaplin himself actually arrived, and being the smallest of the men to emerge, was immediately seized upon by the crowd, who, in one way or other, began to (as they were wont to do in every locale) 'love' him to death. In addition, J.L. Murphy related that at every stop, Chaplin received upwards of fifty letters from 'girls who want to go into the movies or from persons asking financial assistance. In the middle of the night, his telephone may ring several times,'[64] all in the name of fame and fan adoration.

Chaplin's next planned rally was scheduled for 22 April in Greenville, Mississippi, about 152 miles away. Even though the Chaplin party had nine more scheduled rallies after Greenville,[65] they only kept one more and that was in New Orleans on 23 April.[66] As of 21 April, the local organizers plus Carlyle Robinson had not found a venue large enough to house the rally, given the numbers being commanded by other such events. Chaplin's party was to arrive at 2.15 pm from Greenville. The organizers had decided to hold the rally in the evening, with a parade then in the early afternoon.[67] By 22 April, they had decided to hold the event at the Palm Garden at the Fairgrounds, devising special streetcar service out there for convenience. The parade was to start at 2.30 pm featuring Chaplin in an open car with his three companions plus Leslie M. Shaw, former secretary of the treasury. Other features of the parade included a platoon of mounted police, two companies of sailors, two of soldiers, two military bands and two tanks.[68] However, by the actual day of the rally, the parade had been canceled due to Chaplin's poor health. The rally at the Palm Garden, however, would go on.

That evening, the event itself began at 8.00 pm, but was preceded by Emile Tosso's band. W.B. Thompson presided over the rally itself and, indeed, it turned out that they needed the over-large venue, because 10,000 people packed in and signed up $227,000 in subscriptions. Earlier in the day the first speaker, Leslie Shaw, had vocalized his 'expressed sharp disapproval of the country using moving picture actors and actresses in the work of obtaining subscribers to the

Liberty Loan.' Seeing the throng of Chaplin fans moving in waves before him, he realized his mistake too late and spent most of his allotted time trying to gain his audience's attention. With Chaplin's entrance, the crowd went crazy, and the actor spent several minutes pacing the stage and throwing kisses before they calmed down. When he started talking, he had everyone's ear it seemed, giving his usual serious speech which surprised them, both because it was of such a serious camber, and because their silent favorite was speaking to them in his marvelous English accent for the first time. After ten stirring minutes, a man interrupted to:

> claim the right to make the first subscription. Chaplin jumped into the air, seized his derby and did his nifty hat trick. Up into the air he went and his coat came off. The crowd went wild. He jumped into the bandstand and led the playing of *The Stars and Stripes Forever*, going Sousa one better in the art of gesticulation. Back to the stage he came. Three rousing cheers for the army and navy he led and followed it with three more for President Wilson. The noise was deafening.[69]

This same reporter believed Chaplin's event to be the most effective of the Liberty Loan campaign. The aftermath of his speech and antics included the usual endorsing of subscriptions, kissing of children and shaking of hands. A bit different was the Chaplin party's seeming inability to escape these adoring multitudes afterwards. A mob of people surged the platform and policemen had to be called to cut a pathway for Chaplin and company to escape to their awaiting cars. But the night was not quite over, for a special screening had been planned. *A Dog's Life* was just making its rounds and Chaplin had neither seen it in its final edited form or in an actual theater. He was to do so this night at a special screening at 11.00 pm at the Strand Theatre there in New Orleans in private showing.[70]

Although this was Chaplin's last Southern United States Liberty Loan stop, it was not his last appearance for the Liberty Loan Tour itself, for he was present in New York City on 30 April for an event there in Liberty Bell Park. One New Orleans report claimed he would be staying there in the Grunewald Hotel for the interceding week, but then recanted the claim in a later piece, indicating that Chaplin would be leaving on 24 April.[71] The 20th Century Limited, the train Chaplin would have taken cross-country, took two full travel days and three nights to cross the country. Chaplin arrived then in New York on 27 April and was interviewed at length in his room, number 434, at the Ritz-Carlton Hotel by Walter K. Hill, who was permitted to ask Chaplin several questions as the actor dressed for dinner. Chaplin revealed that he hoped to discover the secret to being funny every time, that he was willing and ready to serve his country as a soldier, and that he hoped to finish three more films before he was actually called up. Hill commented to Carlyle Robinson that 'Charlie Chaplin deserves all the good luck a mortal can have, and all the millions he can pile up. He's a regular man.[72]

A long list of events featuring many celebrities in many venues were on the program in New York on 30 April, so Chaplin was just one smallish fish in a much bigger pond. The program included that an artifact called the Liberty Ball was leaving Peekskill at 9.00 am and moving closer towards the big city, that Liberty Land was opening at the 69th Regiment Armory at 11.00 am, that various and sundry patriotic speeches would be given at Liberty Bell Park (really, City Hall Park) at noon (Chaplin's venue, and note that his is not named specifically), that a Dewey Day parade was to be held at 1.00 pm, that a school children's parade to Liberty bank was to be held at 2.00 pm, that an Italian Day celebration was to be held at Washington Arch at 8.00 pm and that a Liberty Loan rally was to be held at the same time at Carnegie Hall. One reporter commented that even though the Liberty Bell Park had filled to overflowing with French and American soldiers before Chaplin arrived there, after they filed out, he simply filled it up again. He 'pleaded with an earnestness which he never displays on the screen for more bond buyers,' announcing to his audience that this appeal would be his last for this effort, as he was leaving that night for Los Angeles. He divulged to them that he had spent $125,000 of his own money on Liberty Loans, more than he could actually afford, asking those within earshot to do the same. 'And such is his power over the human heart and imagination that a satisfying number of persons did,' recalled the same witness.[73] Another reporter heard the total as $400,000 and that Chaplin then asked his audience to do the same by chipping in $50. $400,000 seems like the wrong figure (too much!!) but the rest of what he reported seems more correct.

In talking to the audience for a full hour, Chaplin noted that 'Money is nothing. A few years ago I was broke; I didn't have a nickel. But I was happier than I am now … When I was broke I didn't give a damn what happened and therefore was contented.'[74] But his money-making for the Liberty Loan wasn't quite over even after he'd left the scene. One Horace J. Partridge retrieved Chaplin's shoe that he lost trying to escape the crowd after his speech had ended and put it to work, telling the crowd:

> This is Chaplin's shoe. I picked it up this morning. It is the biggest receptacle I could find, outside of a two-gallon bucket. That's why I kept it. You're going to fill it with silver, and the man whose quarter is the first to overflow – he gets the shoe.

Supposedly the shoe contained $100 as of the article's publication and its total was growing yet.[75] On Wednesday, 1 May, Chaplin made a speech at the Men's restaurant at the Hotel Astor during the lunch hour, where he was introduced by Captain Bealley, a British line officer, who was in the US recovering from wounds he had received on the battlefield in Flanders. He couldn't say enough about all the good Chaplin's comedy films had done for the morale of the

British soldiers, who had 'laughed away their troubles in the little temporary theaters behind the trenches watching Charlie's antics on the screen.'[76] All that was left for Chaplin was to collect his grip and go home. Neither Charles Lapworth nor J.L. Murphy made speeches here, so it seems clear that the party of four had broken apart the week before at some point. Rob Wagner and Chaplin remained friends until Wagner's death in 1942, and Charles Lapworth remained on friendly terms with Chaplin. He may have just decided it was time to seek greener pastures elsewhere, but in any event, he was no longer part of Chaplin's three-man personal assistant team that had helped him create the gags for *A Dog's Life*.

The papers reported Chaplin's official return to Los Angeles as 12 May at 2.40 pm on the Santa Fe, having sold some 50 million dollars' worth of Liberty bonds.[77] He didn't start the new project, No. 2 *Camouflage* as it was first titled, until 27 May, but the Liberty Loan tour and all the cantonments he'd visited along the way had given him lots of material for this next film, so he wouldn't have to troll around looking for a good story, because he already had a good bit of it in mind.

Chapter 3

World War I: *Shoulder Arms* and *The Bond*

When work at the studios started up again on 27 May with three short words, 'talked over gags', for production No. 2 *Camouflage*, later to be titled *Shoulder Arms*, the studio had a new manager: Chaplin's old Karno boss, Alf Reeves, who was smoothly promoted from stage manager. John Jasper had lasted with the Chaplin brothers and the Chaplin *modus operandi* for about one year before he'd had enough and turned in his resignation in a letter addressed to Chaplin in Memphis on 15 April. The problem was finances, as David Robinson and others have already discussed. Jasper needed $3,000 a week to run the studio and pay the salaries of its workers and others. Chaplin was only sending him $2,000 and then begrudgingly, or so the letter suggested, and Jasper just couldn't take it anymore: 'Why don't you put sufficient funds in the Citizens National Bank and stop all this confusion? It is not as if you did not have the money, like so many others.'[1] But this wasn't the whole story, for another document reveals that Jasper then gave official two-weeks' notice to Chaplin in writing on 27 May, meaning he would have left the studios in mid-June, a full month and a half later. But, in fact, he didn't leave then either. There is existing correspondence indicating that he was heavily involved in the shipment of negatives for Chaplin's patriotic film donation to the United States government, *The Bond*, in September 1918. However, it was only a matter of time. The brothers had already decided that the job was Reeves's, and unfortunately, they chose a time when Jasper was off sick to swing the axe. In a letter dated 14 October 1918, written and sent to Jasper by Sydney, his convoluted reasoning and sickeningly compassionate overtures must have made the recipient convulse:

> After going over our financial statements, which are far heavier than we anticipated, it was resolved that a cutting down of overhead expenses would have to be resorted to and as Mr Reeves is in receipt of a substantial salary and has very little to do, it was decided that he should be given the management of the studio in place of yourself.[2]

The logical solution, of course, would have been to lower Reeves's salary or figure out something else for him to do, but that never seems to have been considered. One wonders how Jasper responded.

It really didn't matter how famous they became or how wealthy, Charlie and Sydney Chaplin were creatures of the music hall stage, and they were street urchins. They operated their business the same way. Jasper, as an experienced businessman and manager, just simply couldn't understand their way of thinking. Of course, the Chaplins would never let anyone outside the 'family,' so to speak, have any control over the money, because that person could never be trusted with it. Such a person was akin to the landlord or the bill collector that would kick them out on the street as quickly as look at them. The Chaplin boys had all kinds of experience with those types of people. Perhaps John Jasper was completely trustworthy, but he would never be one of them, so he could never be trusted. Alf Reeves, on the other hand, was 'family.' He'd been through the same hardships as they had; he was a music hall brother and what's more, he understood their business philosophy. He would manage the Chaplin studios until his death in 1946.

As the production reports indicate, Chaplin began filming the Little Tramp in civilian life in what would be the first act of the film, using three male child actors, True Boardman, Jr., Marion Feducha and Frankie Lee, who formed a nice triangle from shortest to tallest when standing next to their father on the street. All were similarly attired as well, but with different hats than their father. The first day's report only lists Boardman and Lee, but obviously Chaplin got smart and added the third boy on the second day when rehearsals started, because three is always better than two. The tramp's fecund and over-worked mate in this act of the film was never seen, only referenced, and from those references the audience understood her to be largish and domineering. Weg, a film critic for the *St. Louis Times*, was graced with access to Chaplin during the filming of this scene and after, thereby providing a rare glimpse of his rationale for the way the characters were presented:

> You see, this chap is a henpecked husband, but as the bullying wife has been worn to a frazzle in the pictures, I tried to get a new angle on her. This one never is seen, but she makes her presence felt. It is in a measure an experiment.[3]

After preparing the food wrongly and doing the washing wrongly and being on the receiving end of a missile of some kind from the wife, Charlie received a piece of mail, which she demanded to open first. It was his draft letter, which he held tight with relief, when he sees it.

Except for 8 June, when work was held up due to an eclipse, and 10 June when there was a blackout, work continued unabated on this act until 14 June, when they shot the last scene outside the Mecca saloon in Venice Beach. The Little Tramp's examination board scene started up the very next day.

June 15 through 20 were taken up with preparing the new act and waiting on the sets to be built. Players in this scene would be Edna Purviance, Albert Austin, Henry Bergman, Tom Wilson, and Jack Young. The Little Tramp goes to the examination board to see Dr. Francis Maud to make sure he's fit to serve. The doctor's name is already ambiguous enough to cause Charlie a little anxiety as to whether or not he might be a she, especially when he sees an image of the doctor through the glazed window of the door and mistakes his headgear for a bun. He takes off (naked by this time, expecting an exam) into a nearby office and realizes that Edna is nearby doing her secretarial job, so he moves from room to room, trying to escape her notice, while trying to hide himself from the audience at the same time. Meanwhile, the doctor begins looking for him because he's not where he's supposed to be. Charlie has gone into yet another room and encounters a second female employee and is now hiding from her, until he finally slides back towards Dr. Maud's office, somehow has his pants on again and is relieved to see that Dr. Maud is in fact a man. The exam begins. The audience witnesses the check-up in chiaroscuro behind the doctor's glazed door window, and what it sees for the most part seems anatomically impossible (Albert Austin played the doctor). A large spoon used to check Charlie's throat is swallowed by accident, as are the pliers used to try to retrieve the spoon. Then Dr. Maud uses a piece of thread to retrieve the pliers, which succeeds, and finally, Charlie coughs up the spoon as well. All very sophisticated music hall trickery. Charlie passes his exam with flying colors.

This act was worked on continuously until the 4 July holiday. Chaplin's former co-star Marie Dressler and her friend Ina Claire visited the studio on 11 July and so there was no work that day. When work resumed, a new act was on the agenda and suddenly the first two acts were thrown on the rubbish heap. Chaplin's plan for a three-act film would now be altered entirely. Instead, he would take the time to expand the last planned act – the Jimmy the Fearless inspired one – into the whole film. In other words, the Little Tramp would fall asleep after some exertion in the first few moments of the film and then most of the action would take place in his dream, from which he would wake up in the very end. The three acts would now be contained within the dream itself: 1) his introduction to daily life in the trenches, 2) volunteering for a secret mission behind enemy lines, and 3) capturing the Kaiser. After all that heroism and glory, of course, the Little Tramp must wake up at the end to find out that none of it had really happened. Now, however, there would be no little boys nor domineering wife in the film.

For the first act in which Charlie becomes acclimated to life in the trenches, the studio set builders constructed a magnificent reproduction of an actual trench in the Chaplin studios swimming pool, thereby allowing the flooding of the trench scenes to happen without much worry. Using newsreel footage as their models, no detail was left out, and even those critics who were not fans of the film usually sung the praises of the trench's authenticity. After demonstrating the ups and downs of daily life in the trench, Charlie and his platoon are told they must go 'over the top in 15 minutes.' It was this scene the company was filming on Tuesday, 23 July, when it was discovered too late that some of the props had been tampered with, targeting Chaplin himself. John Jasper's cable to J.D. Williams on the subject was published in total in the *New York Exhibitor's Trade Review*, due to the seriousness of the incident:

Charlie Chaplin slightly injured during production of war picture. Had number of small cans fastened over trench containing proper amount of powder to make effect of bursting shrapnel. Rehearsed scene before lunch. During lunch time the wires connecting explosives had been tampered with and several lead slugs placed in can directly above where Chaplin goes over the top. Instead of explosions occurring in sequence rehearsed, the one directly over Charlie went off as he was going up ladder at side of trench. Had he been looking up as he was when scene was rehearsed, his sight would have been destroyed, but he dropped bayonet and leaped down to pick it up. He was only saved from serious injury by shrapnel helmet which was struck by two slugs. Chaplin continued with scene and Camera caught the whole episode. It is a noticeable fact that since announcement that

Chaplin was to make a propaganda picture for the U.S. Fourth Liberty Loan, nearly all applying for work in picture have been decidedly Teutonic in appearance and talk. We have been more than careful in employing extras. An armed guard has been placed on the estate and around the studio to prevent further trouble. No one allowed on stage except those essential to scene being made. Chaplin's hands and face slightly burned by burning powder and uniform badly burned. John Jasper.[4]

The production report doesn't mention the incident and filming began at 11.00 am the next day, apparently unimpeded by the incident.

In August, some of the more strenuous scenes in which Charlie and Sydney were sent out on a dangerous mission, Sydney is captured and Charlie camouflages himself in a tree costume were shot on location in Beverly Hills, near Wilshire and Sherman Avenue. *Variety* had already announced on 2 August[5] that the release date for this film was set for 8 September, which seemed overly ambitious at this point. Especially as it was unseasonably hot that August and, on the third, work had to be suspended when the temperatures rose to 108°F.[6] On 7 August, scenes were filmed on the Chateau set. Scenes in Beverly Hills in which Chaplin donned the tree costume and engaged the German soldiers were shot on 9 and 10 August. Forest scenes for this same section of the film were shot on Wilshire on 11 August. Three location scenes were shot on Monday 12 August: 1) the drainage pipe on Sherman Avenue, 2) the big tree also on Sherman and 3) the forest on Wilshire. Interiors of Edna's character's destroyed home were shot on 13 and 14 August, with shooting ending at 1.00 am on the fourteenth. This long night pretty much indicated that Chaplin wanted to finish as much of that part of the film as he could that day, because he had planned to start something else the next work day.

Sure enough, on 16 August, Chaplin and company began work on a propaganda short for the United States government. This is also the first day that the title *Shoulder Arms* appeared on the production report beside the title *Camouflage*, but it did not continue to appear there regularly, for some reason.[7] Such shorts were the 'in' things to do. Some typical examples were Douglas Fairbanks in *Sic 'Em Sam*, Mary Pickford in *100-Percent American*, William S. Hart in *A Bullet for Berlin*, and Allah Nazimova in *A Woman of France*. Actors listed on the production sheet for this first day included Edna Purviance, Albert Austin, Henry Bergman, Tom Wilson, Loyal Underwood, Al Blake, and Otto Brower. Dorothy Rosher, the little blond girl who would perform some antics from the cut-out moon (as Dan Cupid), appeared on the report the second day.[8] After working on this short for three days, 20 August was spent talking story only, which proved fruitful, because the short was completed on Wednesday 21 August.[9] In some ways, this is Chaplin's most modernist or avant-garde film. The sets are white cut-outs on a stark black background. The plot is simple but effective. According to the synopsis provided to the Library of Congress copyright office for what would be # L12955, the title was simply *A Liberty Loan Appeal*, later advertised as *The Bond*. The plot demonstrated four types of bonds:

1) The Bond of Friendship, in which 'Charlie's friend touches him for a loan.' 2) Bonds of Love, in which 'he falls in love at first sight and after being shot by Dan Cupid, becomes all tied up in his love affairs.' 3) Bonds of Marriage, in which they get married. 4) Liberty Bonds, which a) shows Chaplin standing between figures representing Uncle Sam and Industry. Chaplin buys a bond from Uncle Sam and Industry furnishes a soldier with a rifle. Chaplin buys another bond and a sailor is equipped. b) An allegorical figure of Liberty appears. Just as she is about to be cut down by figure representing the Kaiser, he is vanquished by the soldier of Uncle Sam. Then Chaplin hits the Kaiser over the head with a huge mallet bearing the words 'Liberty Bonds' and the picture is ended.[10]

Cutting the picture was completed on 22 August, because the production report for the next two days states that footage of *Shoulder Arms* already taken is reviewed and segregated. Filming of Production No. 2 *Camouflage* (*Shoulder Arms*) resumed then on 26 and 27 August with the scene involving the Kaiser's automobile.

Shooting the ruins of Edna's French home was completed on 28 August. This was also the last day that Melville Brown signed the production reports, perhaps indicating his last day at the studio.[11] The military shots that open the film, before Charlie falls asleep on his cot, and the ones at the end of the film in which Charlie captures the Kaiser and is deemed a hero, were shot at Ross Airfield in Arcadia, California (a World War I air balloon landing field) on 30 August. On 31 August,[12] the cutting of the picture began and continued until 16 September, with retakes being shot here and there as necessary.[13]

In early September, while the film was still being cut, Chaplin felt that he had enough film to make five or six reels and wanted to put feelers out to see if First National would pay for such a film. A questionnaire was put to the First National exhibitors about whether they would prefer the film be three or six reels and 87 per cent voted for three reels. Also, Chaplin was asking $400,000 for the six-reel edition of *Shoulder Arms*, which First National also refused to pay.[14] Then, in a cable to Syd Chaplin from John Jasper, dated 3 September, Jasper claimed that Metro had offered $400,000 for it and Lasky $450,000. He suggested that they might be able to buy the picture back from First National and then sell it to one or the other of these companies, but obviously, it wasn't that simple. The cable ends with 'C C singing.'[15] Obviously, Chaplin was already feeling the constraints of his contract with First National and not liking them. In a 28 September article in *Motion Picture News*, the writer stated that:

Rumors of discontent, disagreements, and difficulties of various descriptions which have been assigned by some elements of the industry as reasons for the intervals between the release of

Chaplin comedies, and the lack of a definite schedule of release dates, will be answered in a statement to be issued . . . from the offices of First National Exhibitors' Circuit on behalf of Mr Chaplin.[16]

So, even though First National had promised Chaplin he could take his time on the films he made under the contract, he was supposed to complete eight in sixteen months and a full year had already elapsed with only two in the hopper, so the speak. Obviously, this was creating a lot of tension for the exhibitors and probably for Chaplin as well. And then there was the Spanish influenza epidemic.

Just as *Shoulder Arms* was to be released, The National Association of the Motion Picture Industry released a statement allowing 'no new or re-issue pictures for a period of four weeks commencing Tuesday, October 15, 1918, and ending Saturday, November 9, 1918. Serials and newsreels will be the only exceptions and may be released as usual.'[17] First National was not a member of the NAMPI, and as Mr Schwalbe explained to the press, could not legislate to its members about what to do. However, he did suggest that it was the company's desire to live up to the 'spirit and intent' of the agreement as much as possible, sending this message out to his exhibitors. Because they did not have set release or schedule dates and may already have had prints of some yet-to-be released films, he asked exhibitors whenever possible to hold new releases until after 9 November.[18] Chaplin's *Shoulder Arms*, however, was not delayed by this mandate and was successfully released on 20 October 1918 at the Strand in New York City for a week, then released to other theaters in the city, then on 4 November in Brooklyn,[19] although release throughout the rest of the country was announced as 27 October.[20]

After the film was released to the public, Chaplin provided a statement to First National about how he had decided to approach what could be a touchy subject:

Military life abounds with possibilities for humor. But to picturize any of them without actually ridiculing traditions, method and purpose proved more than a task. I did not want to get effects which would reflect in the slightest degree upon the service, and still it was necessary to create action that would involve the ordinary daily events of a doughboy's life and make them appear really laughable.

To do this I decided that one central character – a typical 'boob' recruit – could provide the situations by his own stupidity and difficulty in mastering the principles of soldiering and properly draw into the mix-ups representatives of every rank and branch of the service. This idea, carried out in 'Shoulder Arms,' brought the proper result, providing a score of novel situations without detracting in the least from the respectability of soldiery.[21]

And, it was a huge hit, despite the influenza pandemic or anything else. The Strand announced that it would hold the film over for a second week, something it had not done before in its history.[22] S.M. Weller wrote:

Look at his work seriously and there is found in it a method and an art for which he is not given proper credit. How really unique he is, is proved in part by the lamentable failure of his many imitators. Having pronounced mannerisms, it seems easy to copy him, but that it cannot be done successfully has been amply demonstrated time and again. There is but one Chaplin and he is worth all he gets. Witness the capacity audiences at the Strand this week and the roars of laughter.[23]

In another specific example of its popularity, F.V. Fisher of the National Exhibitor's Exchange reported to *Motion Picture News* that *Shoulder Arms* had broken all records of attendance ever set at the Liberty Theatre in Bellingham, Washington. With the local population numbering 25,000, some 14,000 of those saw the film, with the manager of the Liberty writing to Fisher that he simply 'could not handle the crowds.'[24] The answer seemed to be longer booking times for most venues. T.J. Tally, still the owner of the southern Californian and Arizona First National franchises, decided to open a new theater in Los Angeles just to promote longer runs of feature films, something he announced 21 December. With the ban on such construction over with the war, Tally could now bring his plans to fruition. He believed that the film industry was encountering an era of new specialization in productions by such stars as Chaplin, Mary Pickford (signed with First National in mid-November 1918), Anita Stewart (another well-advertised First National star) and others who would release longer films of a much higher quality and, therefore, theater managers could better plan for longer runs of those films and a reduction in program changeover.[25] In essence, Tally would be gambling even more of his own money on Chaplin's ability to come up with yet another hit and another one after that *ad infinitum*, or at least up to the count of the eight he owed with his First National contract. Tally was confident, given the first two, that Chaplin would be able to do that, no matter how much time it took. But he may have been unnecessarily setting himself up for a big fall, or at least a difficult set of challenges to come.

Concurrent with all this success and happiness, Chaplin and his lawyer Nathan Burkan decided to file an injunction against filmmakers Julian Potash and Isadore Peskov in the United States District Court from screening their film *Charlie in the Trenches* at the Crystal Hall Photoplay theater. In addition, Chaplin asked for $50,000 in damages for defamation of character both to himself and his Little Tramp persona brought on by the imitator hired to enact certain scenes, which were edited together with certain patched positives assembled from various releases from his old films. As in the most heinous of imitator cases, Chaplin alleged that his character had taken full form in the Keystone film *Mabel's Strange Predicament* in 1914, describing the persona thus:

> His ill-fitting, much too large and loose and baggy trouser; the large shoes, his shuffling, awkward flatfooted walk; the small hat, the cane, the little mustache, together with the mannerisms, eccentricities, gesticulations, gestures and facial expressions present a most unique, extraordinary and distinctive personality.[26]

This description illustrated by comparison the extreme level of heresy being carried out by the actor imitating Chaplin's persona in his portrayal, thereby demanding the suit. The film, however, obviously had hoped to succeed based on the popularity of Chaplin's current military comedy.[27]

Almost ten years later, the tables were turned when a man named Leo Loeb took Chaplin to court in New York on what Chaplin's lawyer, Nathan Burkan, rightly determined were two distinct and contradictory charges: 1) that Chaplin had plagiarized a scenario of Loeb's personal World War I experience for his film *Shoulder Arms*, therefore he was suing for all profits made from the film, and 2) that Chaplin, in using Loeb's scenario after Loeb had sent it to the Chaplin studios, had an implied contract for the treatment (even though he had received a rejection letter from Melville Brown) and was asking $50,000 payment for the scenario given that implied contract. The trial started on 4 May 1927 and lasted until 15 May 1927,[28] with Chaplin in town anyway due to the divorce from his second wife, Lita Grey Chaplin, and the subsequent backlash.[29]

Leo Loeb was a leather worker by trade and only spent a year and a half as a Marine, serving in World War I. The treatment he sent to the Chaplin studios was only fifteen paragraphs long and he had never written anything before, i.e., he was not a writer. He sent the fifteen paragraphs on 12 April 1918, and received the treatment back on 23 April, with a note enclosed from Melville Brown, the Chaplin studios employee charged with dealing with such things at the time. The note basically stated, 'the scenario had been read, that the idea had been believed to be very good, but that Chaplin had determined at that time not to burlesque the United States service, and, consequently, the scenario was not available for his uses.'[30] After spending his opening statement pointing out to Judge William Bondy the contradictions in the plaintiff's two counts, Chaplin's attorney Nathan Burkan spent 5 May (day 2) cross-examining Loeb on Exhibit A, the fifteen-page scenario in contention, basically trying to prove that every line of it could be any 'rookie' soldier's experience in the war and so, a common experience and not a unique one to Loeb. In other words, it was not one that was so unique to Loeb and his particular scenario that any correlations between it and Chaplin's film would automatically be considered plagiarism. For example, Burkan asked, 'When you say "Charlie passes enlistment office, sees sign and enters," that is a thing that happened to everyone who enlisted?' Loeb answered, 'Yes.'[31]

After he worked through Loeb's treatment, Burkan began moving slowly through the plot description of *Shoulder Arms*, scene by scene with Loeb, asking the plaintiff after describing each scene which elements were in his treatment and which weren't – a very long and laborious process.[32] At about Scene 32, the judge stopped the examination and again brought up to the defense attorney Mr Hays what he saw as the main problem, that a case such as this was normally tried in equity, not before a jury, because it must be proven to be an intellectual product, not a literary one. An intellectual product could not be taken by anyone else legally, but the jury must somehow decide what exactly Loeb did – what he wrote – and then whether Chaplin appropriated that. And so, Burkan continued working through the scenes with Loeb. What he was trying to achieve was to show Loeb that all the little incidents and moments within scenes couldn't possibly have come from his treatment, that a five-word description of a scene like 'Charlie's Regiment Landing in France' could not result in all the convoluted action, such as the flooding of the trench (even the frog on Syd's toe) to Charlie's reading of a soldier's letter over his shoulder when he receives no mail of his own, or his saving Edna from harm at the hand of the Germans in her destroyed home included in the

Chaplin incarnation. Loeb and his attorney, however, reiterated that, in fact, this was exactly what they would have expected Chaplin to do with the skeletal script. As Hays explained on Day 3:

> I will make the further concession that we do not claim that any of those specific incidents, as incidents, appear in our scenario, but merely that the story of our scenario is copied and that those incidents are proper incidents to tell the story of our scenario. Our claim is not as to the specific incidents that Chaplin has adopted in using our story, but in the story itself.[33]

On Monday, 9 May (Day 4), the film was finally shown to the court against Mr Hays's wishes, and then he duly tried to show that his client's short treatment followed the plot point for point, on which even the judge disagreed with him. Burkan's next tactic was to put Carlyle Robinson on the stand for two reasons: as someone from the Chaplin studios who Chaplin used as a sounding board during the Liberty Loan tour regarding ideas for the new film (and who took notes), and as someone who went into the service in June and wrote to Chaplin continually about his 'rookie' experiences there. Burkan also used Robinson's time on the stand to illustrate the many previous literary works in existence that used many similar plot points as those found in the film, placing each one in evidence, to show that their existence in that film was not unique and to keep that in the minds of the jury. Chaplin took the stand next.

It is unclear whether Chaplin's testimony was intentionally obfuscatory, but that was the result. The only date he could remember about the Liberty Loan tour was his own birthday. He could remember who accompanied him somewhat, but not what he discussed with them. He constantly asked for questions to be reframed or restated, because he didn't understand them, he couldn't read the documents because he had forgotten his glasses and he generally created as much chaos on the stand as he could. His description of the way in which he created *Shoulder Arms* and/or the scenario of the film was a nebulous pile of goo that had no meaning. The only piece of information he was sure of was that he had never read or even seen Loeb's treatment.

Following this long two days of testimony was an interesting list of characters who served as witnesses for the defense, including James R. Murphy, who had accompanied Chaplin on the Liberty Loan tour, cartoonist Bruce Bairnsfather, Melville Brown, Syd Chaplin and Thomas Harrington via their depositions taken in 1924, and two members of the publishing community, Charles K. Harris and R.L. Giffen, who was quoted as testifying that Loeb's script 'was not even a scenario, and was, in his opinion, without market value.'[34] This compilation of shenanigans, along with Chaplin's sullied reputation following his nasty divorce from Lita Grey which filled the papers at the same time, most likely led to the deadlocked jury, which came in 10–2 against him and for Mr. Loeb after seven hours of deliberations.[35] However, being deadlocked, Judge Bondy could do little but dismiss the jury and the case – luckily for Chaplin, who had not taken seriously enough an episode he considered to be silly. This was the first of many such plagiarism suits to come in Chaplin's long career.[36]

*   *   *

After *Shoulder Arms* wrapped and well before its release, it became clear that Chaplin was romantically involved with Mildred Harris, a 17-year-old actress he had met sometime in July, supposedly at one of Samuel Goldwyn's parties.[37] This had been bound to happen. With all the time spent away from home being fawned over by strange women and kissed by little girls and boys during the Third Liberty Loan tour earlier in the year, Chaplin had to have turned his thinking to starting a family of his own from time to time, busy as he was. At every stop he had planned activities with children. Back at the studio, his first scene for *Shoulder Arms* engaged three little boys and he added little Dorothy Rosher to the cast of *The Bond*. None of this seems like an accident. Many have speculated that the loss of his first child was the impetus for his writing and filming *The Kid*. There's no doubt it had some influence, but there's a lot of evidence that Chaplin was increasingly interested in starting a family well before that. After all, he was now approaching his thirtieth year.

In *Picture-Play* magazine in December 1918, James J. Tynan wrote begrudgingly about Chaplin's interactions with children at the studios, because it was the closest he was allowed to get to the actor:

> If you have seen a mother hen watching over her chicks, you will have some idea of Charlie Chaplin during the three weeks he had the children working at the studio. A teacher was provided, and Charlie saw to it personally that each child studied a certain number of hours each day. He had the patience of Job with those children, too, for it was warm and they would run off the set to play and get into all sorts of mischief. Everyone else scolded while Mr Chaplin remained unruffled.[38]

When he signed the First National contract, then built his own studio, why wouldn't marriage and fatherhood be logical next steps? That didn't mean, of course, that he would pick the right woman the first time out.

Mildred was visually his type, though: long golden hair, fair, with blue eyes. Mentally, of course, she was immature and no match for Chaplin, who, to be fair, was not well-educated himself, but as a confirmed autodidact, at least was in the habit of surrounding himself with people that could broaden his mind. Mildred wouldn't be one of those people. She announced herself to be pregnant about mid-September and so they married on 23 October 1918, at 7.00 pm at the home of R.S. 'Cupid' Sparks, 2646 S. Normandie Avenue, with the service being performed by Reverend James I. Myers and Chaplin's valet, Tom Harrington, acting as both witness and best man.[39] After swearing the two men to secrecy (the marriage was kept from the press for about two weeks), Charlie and Mildred embarked for a week's honeymoon on Santa Catalina Island. On their return, Chaplin finally gave up his room at the Los Angeles Athletic Club, which he'd occupied since about 1914, and moved into 2000 de Mille Drive in the Hollywood Hills, on a six-month lease. Mildred, who worked under contract for Lois Weber at Paramount, waited for her 'credit rating' to go up when she added Chaplin to her name, which it really didn't. What followed was two plus years of misery for both. The pregnancy that forced the marriage was false, but the real one that followed resulted in a deformed baby (Norman) who lived only three days, caused, Mildred claimed, by the extremely high level of stress in the Chaplin household. Chaplin could not work when Mildred was around – not just' around', but in his life altogether, so Production No. 3, begun formally 4 November 1918, saw Chaplin's first dry spell of his film career, one that made him question his abilities, his sanity and which, of course, ended this first marriage. Only his immersion into his first six-reeler, *The Kid*, which came with problems of its own, would slowly help him out of this funk.

Chapter 4

A Period of Stagnation: Life with Mildred Harris and Severe Creative Blockage: *Sunnyside* (1919), *A Day's Pleasure* (1919) and the formation of United Artists

C haplin had reported to the studio on 4 November 1918 to start work on Production No. 3, tentatively titled *Jack of All Trades*, starting immediately on location at the Phelps ranch outside of Fullerton with the scenes of Charlie moving some cows down a country lane. As Chaplin reported to one inquiring journalist, however, working with animals was not all fun and games:

> In this picture, 'Sunnyside,' we work with animals, and animals get temperamental; a cow even had a pretty, little calf just as we'd gotten out on location, forty miles from town, with a dray-load of props. That spoiled work for the day, and then some of the scenes we thought funniest had to be cut out.[1]

No filming occurred on 7 November, because a 'false' peace was declared and there was a holiday, then again on the 11th, because actual peace was declared and there was a holiday. After these interruptions, shooting moved to the studio and the village main street set that had been built there. Zasu Pitts, a comic actress later well known for comedy films in the 1930s, in which she teamed with actors such as Slim Summerville, Thelma Todd, and James Gleason, was listed on the roster of actors since 4 November and remained there until 24

November when she mysteriously disappeared from the production reports. Although several articles announced her as a new member of Chaplin's company starting directly after the release of *A Dog's Life*, noting her success in Mary Pickford's picture *The Little Princess* the previous November,[2] no footage exists of her ever being part of the this or any other Chaplin production, so it's not clear exactly what happened. A close inspection of the shooting schedule, however, does show that Pitts was filmed acting in the scene at the hotel grocery counter with Charlie on 22 November and then is replaced in the scene by Edna Purviance the very next day, disappearing from the production report the day after that, so perhaps the explanation is very simple: she simply didn't please Chaplin. Syd was listed as part of the shooting schedule at certain points, for instance on 14 November, when he rode 'the wheel,' known as a penny-farthing, towards the church, chasing a goose and then when Charlie enters town on the charging bull, Syd was supposed to plow into him on the wheel, but obviously these parts were removed later, for he doesn't appear in the film at all.

On 15 November the Bishop of Birmingham paid a visit to the studio, thereby causing work stoppage for the day. Some film was shot of the visit (Syd is seen riding the wheel in it, for instance) and the event received some coverage in the papers. The setting moved to the interior of the hotel on 18 November, but no film was shot on that day, for the action was only rehearsed. Chaplin and his team worked on the story for the next few days, resuming the shoot in the hotel interior set on 21 November. Shooting on this set continued until 6 December, except for the Thanksgiving holiday, held that year on 28 November. On the 6th, Chaplin is noted as segregating the film – separating it out and seeing what he had. On the 9th, he began shooting Albert Austin in the barber chair, footage that would be scrapped later, but the next day he was back to working on the story. During 11–13 December, Chaplin was cutting the film, but then the next day he was absent from the studio. On 16 December,

Rollie Totheroh is noted as taking film of a rabbit hopping through the hallway of the empty Evergreen hotel lobby. This was the last work done in the studio in the year 1918 and by 18 January 1919, the production report states that the studio 'closes tonight for an indefinite period.' No shooting had yet been done in 1919, although the studio staff and workers had been receiving pay up to that point. This coincided, of course, with the creation of United Artists and Chaplin's momentary flirtation with dropping his contract. Sam H. Comly reported:

> Charles Chaplin will close his studio in a week and lay off his working force of thirty-one people. Says he is going to Europe to enjoy his honeymoon and will make one picture for First National in England and another in France. J.D. Williams of First National says they are in favor of Chaplin's plans. He says that in addition to the three pictures made by Chaplin that two more are finished waiting to be cut.[3]

An alternative story had been floated by Syd on 13 January that his brother was suffering from a nervous breakdown and would be leaving for Europe to rest, closing the studio to do so. His wife Mildred, having recently recovered from a similar ailment, was needed in Los Angeles on the movie set by her director Lois Weber, so would not accompany him.[4] The fact was that First National had been holding their big meeting in downtown Los Angeles at the Alexandria Hotel the second week of January, and Syd came up with the idea to hire a female detective to snoop around down there and see what she could find out. This suspiciousness was brought on by a few factors: 1) Chaplin had recently requested additional production funds from First National and had been haughtily turned down, 2) both Mary Pickford and Douglas Fairbank's contracts were about to run out and neither had been asked to renew by First National or Famous Players Lasky respectively and 3) there were rumors that First National was suddenly hot to merge with Zukor's Famous Players Lasky and was trying to sign up a bunch of new (to them) big stars beforehand. Syd called a meeting at his house on the Chaplin studio property on 14 January, inviting Charlie, Charlotte Pickford (as a stand-in for an ill Mary), Doug Fairbanks, William Hart, and D.W. Griffith. *The Moving Picture World's* A.H. Giebler recounted the startling results of all this intrigue the next day when he called on Fairbanks at his studio, who seemed extremely over-stimulated for some reason. Syd soon arrived grasping an important paper with three signatures on it, those of Fairbanks, Griffith and Hart.[5] After a short car ride, the three men added Pickford and Chaplin's signatures to the document and at 2.45 pm on Wednesday 15 January 1919, the United Artists was born, and the star system was saved.[6] The stars' statement to the press was as follows:

A new combination of motion picture stars and producers formed yesterday, and we, the undersigned, in furtherance of the artistic welfare of the moving picture industry, believing that we can better serve the great and growing industry of picture productions, have decided to unite our work into one association, and at the finish of existing contracts, which are now rapidly drawing to a close, to release our combined productions through our own organization. This new organization, to embrace the very best actors and producers in the motion picture business, is headed by the following well-known stars: Mary Pickford, Douglas Fairbanks, William S. Hart, Charlie Chaplin and D.W. Griffith productions, all of whom have proved their ability to make productions of value both artistically and financially.

We believe this is necessary to protect the exhibitor and the industry itself, thus enabling the exhibitor to book only pictures that he wishes to play and not force upon him (when he is booking films to please his audience) other program films which he does not desire, believing that as servants of the people we can thus best serve the people. We also think that this step is positively and absolutely necessary to protect the great motion picture public from threatening combinations and trusts that would force upon them mediocre productions and machine-made entertainment.[7]

Thus, Chaplin's announcement to the press. When the European honeymoon didn't materialize, however, he opened back up, a mere ten days later. The studio opened and resumed filming on 28 January[8] on Production No. 4, laying *Sunnyside* aside for the time being. There would be no breaking of the contract. In fact, because Chaplin owed First National another six films, he would be the last of the big four to produce under the United Artists banner, not being able to do so until 1923. Strangely enough, the First National executives had published a detailed account of Chaplin's particular brilliance in working with their contract in *Wid's Daily*, 1 December 1918. In the article, J.D. Williams noted that First National's contract with Chaplin guaranteed little interference from them in the actual production of his pictures. In other words:

> He is an independent manufacturer, owning and operating his own producing company and the studios in which it works. He can take any length of time he feels is essential to quality in his releases. He is free to choose his own stories. He is not harassed by telegrams and long-distance telephone calls, urging haste in the completion of a picture to make a certain release date.[9]

This article was certainly written in response to two articles that appeared previously focused on Chaplin himself, both in different periodicals published 5 October 1918 in which he offered this statement in response to exhibitors who were clamoring for more and sooner: 'Each Chaplin release has got to have in it the very best work of which I am capable. Comedy situations are much more difficult to work up than the action of dramatic scenes.'[10] Then Williams, on 3 February, sent a cable to Chaplin indicating that if Chaplin could deliver Production No. 3 close to the quality of the first two, he could promise that during the annual meeting of the First National Exhibitors in April, the members would 'readjust your contract satisfactorily.'[11] This was followed one week later by a four-page letter in which Williams hoped to drive home the point that quality was all important to this next, and to every, Chaplin production going forward: 'Sixteen hundred feet of the same Chaplin quality which is such a striking feature of "Shoulder Arms" will be a boon to you and me.'[12] He promised Chaplin that submitting a film of this quality (No. 4) would guarantee that he could 'give you more money for your productions than is specified in the present contract,'[13] following the annual meeting in April, where he was sure he could sway the other members to such a change, especially if Chaplin himself would attend the meeting. Page two of the letter was a list of questions beginning with, 'Do you know that…', all of which provided Chaplin a huge list of reasons why *Shoulder Arms* was such an incredible film and, therefore, why First National hoped to repeat the phenomenon. Page three insisted that the 'vast good will [of the people] is your tribute' and therefore, he must not trifle with it. Finally, Williams cautioned Chaplin not to forget his millions of adoring fans, by providing them 'uninterrupted continuation of quality, consistent, unfailing and positive in its finished form.'[14] This correspondence was to prove a sort of last-ditch effort in this vein for Williams. Chaplin may have failed to respond substantively, but he certainly didn't attend the First National Annual meeting and, what's more, Williams was soon to attempt a sort of merger with the as yet untried United Artists; when that fell flat, it soured the relationship with Chaplin from that point until the eighth film was finally submitted.

Production No. 4. was tentatively titled *Putting It Over*. Eventually to become *A Day's Pleasure*, it was to undergo four incarnations and as many titles before it became the film that was finally released. The first, *Putting It Over*, was begun at the end of January and continued when possible until 21 February. Rain delayed some shooting, so the story was talked over, then everybody traveled to San Diego for the Air Circus there and some footage was even taken on location. On 4 February, the day was spent shooting a scene for *Sunnyside* again, but they were back working on No. 4 the very next day and continued through 21 February, when Chaplin started cutting the film. Interestingly, although none appear in the final film, several days appear to use rig and saddle horses and cowboys. It's clear that this film was nowhere near its final form at this point.

Meanwhile, United Artists was becoming more organized. The counsels for the four actors together wrote the contracts that established the corporation, which would be based in New York and named United Artists, all signed into existence on 5 February 1919. William Gibbs McAdoo, former Secretary of the Treasury, and son-in-law to Woodrow Wilson, well known to Pickford, Fairbanks, and Chaplin due to his instigating the four Liberty Loan tours and their participation in them, was asked to be president of the company, which he declined, but suggested a post as corporate counsel, if they would offer the presidency to his colleague, Oscar Price. All readily accepted. Hiram Abrams was hired as general manager.[15]

A week later, First National's J.D. Williams responded with an interview on the Big Four Combine, as it was called, in *The Moving Picture World*. First off, he strongly objected to the reports that suggested First National had been moving towards a merger with Adolph Zukor's Famous Players Lasky:

> Overtures looking to an amalgamation were made to First National several months ago. We listened to the proposals, which were immediately referred to the circuit members. Their unanimous opinion was that First National's open market policy had nothing in common with the distribution methods of the concerns from which came the suggestions for a merger.[16]

Williams agreed that the stars had taken the best route possible
to ensure an open market for their pictures given the information
they had been given (falsely, he argued) and he praised them for
it. The merger rumors were designed to keep First National from
signing other stars. The formation of UA was unintended fallout
from this strategy and negatively affected both sides. United Artists'
certificate of incorporation was filed with Delaware's secretary of
state on 17 April 1919, with a board of directors consisting of Albert
Banzhaf, Nathan Burkan, Dennis O'Brien, Charlotte Pickford, and
Oscar Price.[17] Fairbanks's first film for UA would be *His Majesty,
the American*, released on 1 September 1919, Griffith's was smash
hit *Broken Blossoms* released 20 October 1919, and Pickford's was
Pollyanna, released 18 January 1920. McAdoo and Price turned out
to be bad bets with little backbone for the business and lost their
jobs within months. Dennis O'Brien easily stepped into the corporate
counsel position he was already doing anyway, and Abrams was fast
elected president.[18]

It was about this time, after the United Artists deal was set in stone,
that Syd decided to leave his brother's employ and set out on his own.
Charlie had just received a letter from Harry Schwalbe approving his
request for an extension of time to complete the eight films required
by his contract, so he was set for a while.[19] Syd wanted his own film
contract and he wanted to own his own airline. He achieved both
for a while and failed at both, running home to La Brea with his tail
between his legs in time to act in Chaplin's final two First National
films, *Pay Day* and *The Pilgrim*. The time apart proved difficult but
necessary for both brothers. Syd won a contract with Paramount
supposedly for twelve pictures, but the first one was so ambitious,
with filming on location in France where there were still no supplies
for film companies or anything else that it went way over budget
and his contract ended in bitter defeat. He started the Syd Chaplin
Aircraft Corporation in 1919 with World War I pilot Emery Rogers,
the first domestic airline in the United States and then closed it in

complete and utter bankruptcy a year later.[20] Charlie, for his part, did his best to complete two meager films in 1919, spent 1920 and 1921 creating a masterpiece and 1922 completing the last three films of his contract. The younger Chaplin fared better but still had a rough time.

26 February 1919 also turned out to be an auspicious day for Chaplin. He attended Max Eastman's 'Hands off Russia!' speech at the Trinity Auditorium that evening in the company of Rob Wagner, who introduced Eastman to Chaplin after the event. The next day, Eastman was invited to tour the Chaplin studios and the two men developed an instant rapport that was to last many years, even as Eastman went from staunch Socialist to conservative Republican later in life. Although Eastman resided in Croton, New York, he was deeply involved with budding actress Florence Deshon, which brought him out to Hollywood on occasion, as did his proselytizing. When he returned to Hollywood in September 1919 and introduced Chaplin to Deshon, the three became inseparable, their parlor games – charades and a speech-making game Eastman had created – developed into full-blown spectacles each night, requiring so much time, energy, and creativity that no one involved had much energy left for work the next day. This spate of game-playing ended when Eastman returned to New York in December 1919, to be continued later. One aspect of this that continued, however, was the spark of a relationship between Chaplin and Deshon.[21]

On 4 March, J.D. Williams attempted a merger with United Artists and sent out another four-page letter with the proposal to all parties involved: Chaplin, Douglas Fairbanks, John Fairbanks, Mary Pickford, and D.W. Griffith. Essentially, what he hoped to do was to bring United Artists into the First National fold, even into the very building in New York that housed its offices. He wished to distribute the films that United Artists produced under its banner – a ridiculous notion, for, as John Fairbanks frankly noted in his response, the whole reason for forming United Artists was for the combine to distribute their films themselves: 'I hardly think the artists would enter into a contract such as you suggest, as I believe their basic idea, in forming their own association, was to be free and independent of any distributing or producing corporations, which have other artists to exploit.'[22] This response and Williams's general inability to achieve this merger seemed to create a downturn in his relationship with Chaplin that only became worse over the remaining years of the contract. Gone now were the offers of more money and more time. Chaplin himself would have to ask for time extensions and contract alterations through his lawyers.

Additional evidence of the general distrust between First National and Chaplin – from Chaplin's side – was contained in a letter from Harry Schwalbe responding to Chaplin's attorney, Arthur Wright, on 5 March, accusing First National of arbitrary cutting of *Shoulder Arms* on two different occasions, which Schwalbe was completely denying. He had received the accusatory letter on 24 February 1919. The first accusation was that the dream sequence had been removed from the film before it was shown at the Strand in New York. The second was that a theater on Hollywood Boulevard had removed the scene with the drainpipe. Schwalbe assured Wright that both cases would be investigated fully. Also, Chaplin had requested to be furnished with any paperwork regarding foreign copyrights, which Schwalbe stated his contract did not require, but that he would consider in the future.[23]

Filming resumed on *Sunnyside* on 25 February, or, more accurately, work resumed, because initially new locations needed to be found. On 26 February and 6 March Chaplin was off ill, and on 14 March a gale blew down from the hills and caused $7,000 worth of glass damage on the Chaplin stage.[24] On 9 March, press releases appeared that gave some indication of what to expect of Chaplin's next First National effort, but the description was still very vague: '"Sunnyside" shows the picturesque rural life of the average New England village community. Chaplin's satire of the farmhand is said to be his best work and besides the members of his company, he used for foils livestock of every description.'[25] By 18 March, however, they were filming in the parlor set, Edna's parlor, where she entertained the 'new' man in town as well as Charlie. Filming between 25 and 31 March was done on the hotel lobby set, including the bedroom and kitchen, scenes in which Charlie is rudely awakened by his boss, played by Tom Wilson, cooks breakfast, and gets his day started. On 1 April, Chaplin and company began shooting the scene in which Charlie falls off a bridge and has the dream of dancing with the nymphs, in a little homage to Nijinsky. This was filmed on San Fernando Road bridge and took five days. Back at the studio on 6 April, Chaplin was filming on the village street set and Edna's parlor once again. It was only at this late date that Park Jones,[26] the city boy who has a car accident, became part of the plot and the parlor and other scenes were filmed with him. On 9 April, besides those two sets, Chaplin also filmed on a country road in Beverly Hills – the envisioned suicide scene, unique to this particular Chaplin film, for there was never another one. On 14 April, he found the final location he needed: the Lasky ranch, which doubled for the exterior of Edna's house, which was needed to show Charlie's entrance skipping with flowers. Elsie Codd, one of the few journalists, if not the only one, who wrote occasionally about Chaplin's method, because she was actually on his payroll, offered a rare glimpse into the filming of this scene:

Scene 27 (45 feet)
Close-up
Edna's house with garden – marguerites growing beneath window – garden gate closed – Charlie enters[27] from back, running – coat buttoned – he vaults gate, then opens and carefully closes it – tiptoes to window – picks hastily a bunch of the marguerites – then looks cautiously through window.

...

Charlie took that scene five times before the idea occurred to him to add the little bit of funny business with the gate, and he repeated that episode three times because there are infinite possibilities even in closing a garden gate.

The film was then officially completed on 15 April.[28]

The finished product was a three-reel film that was released to the public on 15 June 1919; by the 4 July weekend, the failure of the film was changing the film business and creating predictions of a dark future for film syndicates and production combines if more attention was not paid to the product being distributed. *Sunnyside* was just one of many films that suffered walkouts during the April, May, and June of 1919, but it was definitely the one that took the brunt of the blame for this trend:

> Everyone knows that Chaplin's admirers are worldwide, and that captious criticism or envy never enters into the judgment of the world's millions eager to roar at a universally comic idol, but not all the affection of all the comedian's followers could stem the admission everywhere that 'Sunnyside' should never have been written, never touched, and never circulated, save possibly as a rube drama. No one has yet been found who thinks it is funny unless, possibly, the picture's surely stage-blind producers.[29]

What followed for Chaplin was the threat of oversight on the part of the First National leadership. This is suggested by a response to Chaplin's attorney Arthur Wright from First National treasurer Harry Schwalbe dated 20 November 1919, in reference to the delivery of Production No. 5., eventually titled *The Kid*, which Chaplin wished First National to pick up in Los Angeles, rather than deliver to Chicago as usual. Schwalbe references a comment Wright has made in his letter, however, that 'you are unwilling to permit us to screen the films before they are delivered to us.' He states that he is surprised about this, that he will not insist upon such a screening, because he assumes the film will be in accordance with the contract, but that:

while the contract does not in express terms provide for a screen examination, we think beyond question such right is clearly given by necessary implication, and while we do not insist on that right with regard to the fifth picture, we do not waive it with regard to the succeeding pictures.[30]

It appears that Chaplin has come away from the failure of *Sunnyside* without too much tacit interference from First National as yet, at least in 1919.

But not everyone found the film so terrible. T.E. Oliphant of the *New York Mail* found the film tended a little more toward melodrama than he would have liked, that it was a little uneven, and that 'it is only through the remarkable skill of Mr Chaplin that a series of more or less unrelated incidents in the life of a village drudge are held together with a semblance of what film folk call continuity.'[31] Other critics reported an affinity (as did Oliphant) for the dancing nymphs and the picturesque rural scenes of Charlie herding cattle.[32] Tom Hamlin of *Motion Picture News* gave perhaps the most frank accounting of the film, remarking on its poor supporting cast, bad directing and continuity, but praising the 'fairy girls' and the plenty of laughs throughout: 'This picture is sure to draw heavily everywhere, regardless of where the theater is located. No question about that. Not because it's "Sunnyside," but because it is Chaplin.'[33] The city of Detroit, Michigan reported record crowds for the film which ran for a full week, being booked in 102 houses throughout the metropolitan area and despite a heat wave.[34] Clearly, the bleak aspect the writer for *Variety* wished to place on the issue was not widely held, at least for the present.

What the film did do, however, was create a lot of speculation in the industry press about Chaplin's financial stability at present and in the future. Whereas his Mutual Films contract had paid all production costs and provided him a studio besides, paying him a flat $10,000 a week with a bonus of $50,000, First National paid no production costs and Chaplin built his own studio with his own money. First National paid him per film and per reel of film only. So, in 1918, for instance, he had produced only two three-reel films, for which he was paid $140,000 each, meaning that was his income for the year. His outlay included not only production costs for the films, but several hundred thousand dollars to build the new studio. An article in *Variety* dated 18 July 1919, surmised that the Big Four (the newly formed United Artists) would likely do what they could to help Chaplin out financially in order to 'rush the remaining five of the million-dollar series through,'[35] thereby placing the Chaplin product under the UA umbrella all the sooner. There is no evidence, however, that this was ever even considered.

Putting It Over resumed filming 22 April and then again on 24 April. On the first day, filming was done in the laboratory at the studio with Chaplin, Edna, Albert Austin, Tom Wilson, Charles Levin, and William Hinkley. The next filming day, there was a longer list of cast members, including the four nymphs from *Sunnyside*, Henry Bergman, Loyal Underwood, Tom Wood, J. Redmond, as well as the other cast members from 22 April, but the location was the men's dressing room and the swimming tank at the studio. These two days of filming sound like they include scenes that are now part of what is known as *How to Make Movies*, so perhaps this was Chaplin's vision for Production No. 4. initially. If so, that soon changed.

The second incarnation of Production No. 4 was titled *Charlie's Picnic* and production officially began on 21 May by rehearsing the children, who were initially (as listed on the production reports) Marion Feducha and True Boardman from *Shoulder Arms*, Bob Kelly, and Raymond Lee (who would later appear in *The Kid*). Shooting with the Ford automobile took place until 25 May. Elsie Codd, Chaplin's British publicist, arrived on 24 May and started to work the next day. Shooting of this film ceased on 27 May until 30 June, but so much of importance was to happen between these dates which would affect the film, but, more importantly, would open the door to Chaplin's first feature, probably much sooner than even he would have expected.

Between 15 April, when *Sunnyside* had wrapped and 21 May, when *Charlie's Picnic* half-heartedly began, Chaplin had seen Jackie Coogan at the Orpheum in his first stage appearance. For a week in May 1919, while Coogan, Sr was appearing as an assistant to the great swimming legend Annette Kellerman at the Orpheum Theatre in San Francisco, 4-year-old Jackie would join his father on stage and do the shimmy. This was a lascivious, all-over quake that, being suggestive in nature, was all the more ludicrous and absurd when performed with full vigor by the unknowing youngster. Chaplin had attended the Kellerman show with popular showman Sid Grauman in Los Angeles. In addition to dancing the shimmy, Coogan, Sr would ask Jackie to recite from actor David Warfield's speech in the Broadway hit play *The Music Master*, a performance that Chaplin witnessed.

Production on *Charlie's Picnic* resumed on 30 June – the scene with the car stuck in tar entitled 'the Bullock's set', most likely because it was near Bullock's Department Store located at 3050 Wilshire Boulevard. But as Elsie Codd related the story, although Chaplin planned to shoot both on location at Wilshire and at the studio in a set he had made to look just like it, he eventually decided just to shoot at the studio for the sake of convenience. On a specified day, a call was put out for everyone with a car to show up to the studio with it and about fifty people did so. Codd related that Chaplin 'rehearsed all the traffic business first, substituting the owners for the cars, and getting them to walk through their parts in the literal sense of the word, till their entrances and exits were timed to the minute.' Only then was the traffic cop brought into the scene and actual vehicles were moved around, creating 'a veritable triumph of directorial technique.'[36] Shooting continued apace until the 4 July holiday, then started up again on 9 July.[37] A person would have no idea that Chaplin, filming this scene, had just become a father for the first time, and not only that, but that his new baby was in danger. Needless to say, this was the last day of filming for some time.

Two days before, 7 July, Chaplin's wife Mildred had given birth to a son, Norman Spencer, but he died just three days later.[38] This deeply sad event was believed to have inspired him to make a film with a child co-star,[39] and very soon after, he arranged a meeting with Jackie and his family at the Alexandria Hotel and spent the evening talking to the child. Chaplin was impressed with the boy's intelligence and took away one of Jack's particular responses to a question about what he 'did': 'I'm a prestidigitator who works in a world of legerdemain' – certainly an intriguing response to receive from a soon-to-be-5-year-old. By 28 July, Chaplin had signed young Jackie and his name can be found on the production reports for the film that became *A Day's Pleasure* starting on that date. The production reports for 28 and 29 July also mention the addition of 'Baby Hathaway,' who is well known as the baby used in the first scenes of *The Kid*. A film initially entitled *The Waif*, this film would feature Jackie in a major role and become Chaplin's first feature, a masterpiece that would awaken him from the doldrums, cause him even more problems with First National and allow him to realize that all of that didn't matter, because he would get through the contract, begin making pictures for United Artists and never look back.

So, on 14 October, filming of Production No. 4, now entitled *The Ford Story*, began again out at San Pedro harbor filming on a boat named 'The Ace.' Heavy character actress Babe London had been brought into the cast as Tom Wilson's significant other and a great foil for Chaplin, and Jackie Coogan – now hired in his starring role in Chaplin's other project, tentatively titled *The Waif* – played one of the boys now, with Marion Feducha playing the other. Although Tom Wood, the Eric Campbell substitute who had a role in *Sunnyside*, was originally used as Charlie's wife for the film, Edna Purviance was now cast in the role and would keep it.[40] A four-piece African American band was employed as the dance band on the boat, consisting of John

Williams, E. Sorral, J.A. Irvin and C. Allen. There are some great photos in the archive of Purviance helping to make up the men for their performance. Of course, part of the humor on anything having to do with a boat on water for Chaplin must involve *mal de mer*, which indeed infects nearly everyone onboard, even though they're probably only floating a mile or two offshore from the San Pedro harbor. For the black men, Chaplin chose to have them turn white when they became sick, a rather unfortunate effect that hasn't aged well for obvious reasons. They rented the craft for six days, 14–19 October, to shoot this section of the film and 19 October was considered the completion date for the film.[41]

After all was said and done, the film was renamed *A Day's Pleasure*, was two reels in length and was released on 15 December 1919. *Motion Picture News* described it as unique in Chaplin's oeuvre in that the Little Tramp is characterized as a father with two little tikes and a dimpled darling wife who finds out that a day out might be the most difficult day of the week: 'The family journeys forth to the river where it joins a merry excursion. A rough voyage, a negro jazz band, hot buttered popcorn and a typical Charlie Chaplin fight are some of the incidents'[42] that make up this particular day of pleasure for all involved. The Strand in New York, always the first house to screen Chaplin films, hosted the preview showing on 7 December, which boasted capacity houses at both showings,[43] surely a good sign for the film. Critics overwhelmingly felt that Chaplin had reverted to his old style of comedy in this film – a good thing – but were disappointed that it seemed to end so abruptly. Perhaps the film's greatest praise came from an editorial published in the *Chicago Tribune* during the film's run there, which stated in grand terms that Charles Chaplin 'salvation of us masses … With Mr Chaplin in the arena, we knew that the republic was safe, and lean and hungry Cassius could not plot successfully against the security of principles and institutions necessary to the well-being of the American nation.'[44]

Chapter 5

Betting on *The Kid* (1921): The First Feature Comedy with both a 'Laughter and a Tear'

A couple of weeks before the onset of the new year, J. D. Williams once again received a multiple-page interview in *Motion Picture News* to explain the latest developments for the First National Exhibitors Circuit. The title, 'The Coming Revolution in Filmland,' suggested something major, but Williams seemed to be announcing only a merger with more exhibitors that hadn't been a part of the circuit before. These included Harry Crandall and his eight Washington, D.C. theaters, Charles E. Whitehurst and his six Baltimore theaters and so on and so on, with Williams repeating 'a revolution is abroad in filmland. Exhibitors are the torch bearers.'[1] Perhaps the greatest significance of this for Chaplin and his efforts was that First National was becoming more powerful and would be less and less likely to cater to the needs and desires of one star when it possessed the contracts of many. While *A Day's Pleasure* in some ways made up for the disappointing *Sunnyside*, Chaplin was in no position to be trying something new or to be considering a feature that took him outside the confines of his contract. But, from 31 July 1919, or thereabouts, that was exactly what he was doing, regardless of the consequences. He had been wanting to make a picture with the Little Tramp in tandem with a child for some time, so when he found Jackie Coogan by chance, he knew he had found *the* child and that opened the floodgates of the creativity that had been pent-up inside of him for some time. This film would take some time, which he knew would cause more problems with First National, but he had to find a way to work around that. The film would take exactly one year, the longest Chaplin had ever taken on a project.

Baby Hathaway had been chosen to play little Jackie as an infant in the opening scenes of the film and Chaplin began shooting these in late July, using locations on Pickford Street, Alameda Street, and an alley set devised at the studio. The 7 and 9 August were spent filming lodging house scenes and then attention was moved to the attic set on the lot starting 18 August, after many days of not shooting at all. A notice appeared in the production reports on this day that a 'new version beginning today', and that everything shot before would be discarded, so in that case, Chaplin's initial filming involved the attic set up until 30 August, when some shooting was also done at 415 Ducommun Street in downtown Los Angeles.

After Labor Day, one final day was spent in the attic set, followed by two days of no shooting and then a move to the street set at the studio, which on 5 September is referred to as 'street set – slums.' Given the cast list, this is the scene in which it is discovered that, small as he is, Jackie can fight, and is placed opposite the much larger boy played by Raymond Lee. Unfortunately for Chaplin, it was announced on Friday, 12 September, that his wife Mildred had accepted a contract with First National Exhibitor's Circuit, with Louis B. Mayer producing her pictures. Although there is no direct evidence on or near this date of his reaction, having Mildred's fortunes dependent on the same company as his own had to have caused some consternation on Chaplin's part and may have led to some of the many avoidable situations that were to occur in the coming months. If nothing else, it would have played upon his growing distrust of First National, made stronger by the discernible downturn in his relationship with J.D. Williams, a relationship that would only continue to decline.

Shooting on *The Waif* continued on the attic set until 17 September, when it is noted that Jackie was 'lost and licked.' One account of this incident offered that Jackie had become attached to an older boy named Fields who was an experienced swimmer, which Jackie was not. So, on this day, when Chaplin was involved coaching another boy for a change, Jackie took off:

It came to the time when he used Jackie and he looked around and he couldn't find him. Searched all over and hollered 'Jackie, Jackie!' His mother and dad came running and searched all over the place – out to the front to see if he was out there. Finally, Charlie said, 'I wonder if he could have fallen in that pool.' So we got ahold of Fields. He went diving down to the bottom of the pool to see if he could find [...] him and all of a sudden, he appeared and he had some sort of a garment in his hand. We thought sure it was Jackie. Then we called up the police and they were searching all around; this must have taken about an hour and a half. Finally, a little head peeked from behind the set, laughing his head off. We said, 'Well, where have you been, Jackie?' He said, 'Oh, I've been watching you all the time and getting a kick out of it.' Of course, we took him in the room and spanked the hell out of him.[2]

Shooting on the street set picked up again the next day and continued until 24 September, when some filming occurred on location in Chinatown. Then a couple of days of rain shut down production and when it resumed, Chaplin seemed to be on another tack entirely, filming on a flop house set for three days from 30 September to 2 October in what has come to be known as 'The Professor,' given away in the production notes by the words 'flea bus' or flea business. This at a standstill, Chaplin talked story for a few days, then decided to return to *Charlie's Picnic*, which he now wanted to call *The Ford Story* and completed filming on 19 October with the San Pedro boat scenes, quickly cutting it together and submitting it to First National for release on 15 December 1919.

Filming on Production No. 5, now titled *The Kid* on the production reports, resumed on 14 November with the street set, but Chaplin reverted to filming the scenes outside the church the very next day and for the next four days. On 20 November, shots of the exterior of the rich home were taken and filming on the Pasadena bridge where Edna contemplates suicide began and continued until 24 November. Albert Austin was noted 'finished' on 22 November and so ended a long run as one of Chaplin's stalwart company of players.[3] Rain and the Thanksgiving Day holiday postponed further filming until the 29th, when filming on location at Hall's Grocery Alley (Chinatown and Mexican quarters) began and continued for three days. After one day back at the studio, scenes were filmed on location at Sunset Park on 4 December. Back at the studio and after two days' postponement due to rain, filming in the attic set began again on 8 December through to the 20th, with welfare officer Frank Campeau's scenes being shot on 15 December. Jackie left for San Francisco to celebrate the Christmas holiday on the 22nd, so work stopped until the 29th, when scenes were shot in the M.P. Alley and Chase Alley in the Mexican town until 31 December, when the studio closed for the New Year's holiday, but were back on Olvera Street, 600 N. Main, and a nearby alley on 2 January 1920.

The 6th through 9th January were spent on the attic set at the studio once again and then on 10 January, Edna's flat was filmed. The 14th through 23rd January Chaplin spent cutting the film to see what he had and probably to give himself time to see where he was going with it. On 28 and 30 January, retakes were done on the street set. On 2 February, tests were done on Purviance, they were back in the attic set the next day and on the street set the day after that; on 5 February they were in the reception set (the police department reception area) for four days, with clouds only being shot on 9 February. Exteriors of the Stimson residence, located at 825 W. Adams and Western were shot between 11 and 13 February. Between 16 and 18 February the scene in the studio of the artist (played by Carl Miller), who the audience comes to recognize is Jackie's father in the film, was shot. Around this time, Chaplin's attention was distracted by having

Chaplin (middle) between two Hawaiian girls, October 1917. (*From the archives of Roy Export Co., Ltd.*)

Chaplin and Rob Wagner on board the S. S. *Matsonia* bound for Hawaii, October 1917. (*From the archives of Roy Export Co., Ltd.*)

A scene from 'How to Make Movies' shot in early 1918. Left to right: Tom Wilson, Loyal Underwood, Henry Bergman, two unknown women, Chaplin, Jack Wilson, Edna Purviance and unknown on the Chaplin stage. (*Copyright ©Roy Export Co. Ltd.*)

Chaplin surveying the progress on his new Chaplin Studios, 1917. (*Copyright ©Roy Export Co. Ltd.*)

Chaplin high up in one of his own trees on the Chaplin Studios lot, 1917. (*Copyright ©Roy Export Co. Ltd.*)

Canoeing on the Chaplin Studios pool, with the dressing rooms visible in the background, 1918. (*Copyright ©Roy Export Co. Ltd.*)

The front façade of the Chaplin Studios under construction, 1917. (*Copyright ©Roy Export Co. Ltd.*)

Syd and Charlie Chaplin looking over the blueprints of the Chaplin Studios, 1917. (*Copyright ©Roy Export Co. Ltd.*)

Debut First National advertisement, January 1918.

The cast of the employment office scene in *A Dog's Life*, 1918. Top left Henry Bergman and Loyal Underwood. Top right James Kelley, second from right. Chaplin front, third from left. (*Copyright ©Roy Export Co. Ltd.*)

Chaplin leading a
military band, Third
Liberty Loan tour,
April 1918. (*From the
archives of Roy Export
Co., Ltd.*)

Chaplin, left, in costume for the final scene of *Shoulder Arms*, Ross Balloon Field, Arcadia, California, 1918. (*Copyright ©Roy Export Co. Ltd.*)

Syd and Charlie Chaplin (middle two figures) in costume for *Shoulder Arms*, Ross Balloon Field, Arcadia, California, 1918. (*Copyright ©Roy Export Co. Ltd.*)

Third Liberty Loan Chaplin car, Nashville, Tennessee. Left to right: Unknown, Chaplin, Rob Wagner, Charles Lapworth, and two unknown men. 18 April 1918. (*From the archives of Roy Export Co., Ltd.*)

Between scenes of *The Bond*. Chaplin looking off to the left, Henry Bergman as Uncle Sam and Syd Chaplin as the Kaiser, 1918. (*Copyright ©Roy Export Co. Ltd.*)

Scene in *The Bond*, Chaplin and Edna Purviance, 1918. (*Copyright ©Roy Export Co. Ltd.*)

Syd Chaplin and Charlie in a scene from *The Bond*, 1918. (*Copyright ©Roy Export Co. Ltd.*)

Chaplin signing the title card to *Sunnyside*, to guarantee authenticity, 1919. (*Copyright ©Roy Export Co. Ltd.*)

Chaplin in costume in a cut scene from *Sunnyside*, 1919. (*Copyright ©Roy Export Co. Ltd.*)

Charles Riesner, Edna Purviance and Chaplin in a scene from *The Kid*, 1921. (*Copyright © Roy Export S.A.S.*)

The First National exhibitors' visit to the Chaplin Studios, with Chaplin in the middle, Jackie Coogan directly behind him and Lillita McMurray (Lita Grey) in front of him, 17 March 1921. (*Copyright ©Roy Export Co. Ltd.*)

Delivering the print of *The Kid* to First National, 30 December 1921. Left to right: Unknown, Sol Lesser, Alf Reeves, Chaplin, unknown, Syd Chaplin. (*Copyright ©Roy Export Co. Ltd.*)

Cut scene from *The Idle Class* at the bowling alley. Left to right: Loyal Underwood, Chaplin as the rich husband, Henry Bergman, 1921. ()

Fancy dress ball scene from *The Idle Class* with Mack Swain, Chaplin and Edna Purviance visible in the foreground, 1921. (*Copyright © Roy Export S.A.S.*)

Chaplin and playwright Edward Knoblock aboard the S. S. *Olympic* bound for Britain, September 1921. (*From the archives of Roy Export Co., Ltd.*)

Chaplin in Berlin, Germany meeting Pola Negri (shown center with her arm through a man's left arm). Chaplin second from right. October 1921. (*From the archives of Roy Export Co., Ltd.*)

Scene from *Pay Day* with Edna Purviance (back to camera) and Chaplin, 1922. (*Copyright © Roy Export S.A.S.*)

Scene outside the Bachelor's Club, *Pay Day*, Syd Chaplin at the left, 1922. (*Copyright © Roy Export S.A.S.*)

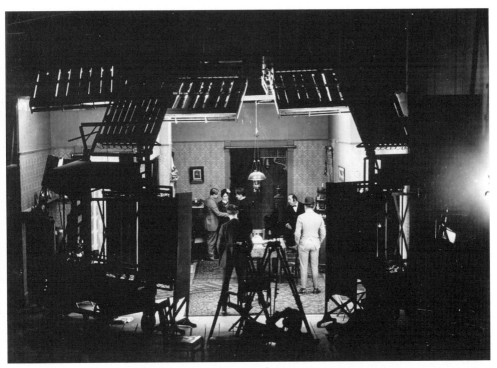

Filming *The Pilgrim*, the scene inside Edna's dining room. Syd Chaplin, May Wells, and Chaplin in a little group at the back left, Mack Swain and Chuck Riesner (back to camera) at right, 1922. (*Copyright ©Roy Export Co. Ltd.*)

On the set of Edna's parlor in *The Pilgrim*. Syd Chaplin in the back holding hat, Chaplin front center next to Elsie Janis on his left, 1922. (*Copyright ©Roy Export Co. Ltd.*)

Carl Miller (left) and Chaplin as director, *Woman of Paris*, 1923. (*Copyright ©Roy Export Co. Ltd.*)

received a speeding ticket for driving 45 miles per hour in a residential zone. On 18 February, he failed to show in court and Judge Walter Handy issued a bench warrant for him,[4] but by 20 February the case had been dismissed, a fact actually noted on the production report for that day.

On 20 January, in the midst of this production, French comedian Max Linder arrived back in Hollywood for a second try at success in the United States. He had met Chaplin, the American comedian with whom he had the most affinity, back in 1917 when he moved out to Hollywood under the Essanay Studios banner. He traveled back home to France late that year, after suffering a relapse of his old lung malady, most likely tuberculosis. This time, he would negotiate distribution of his films as he made them, all under the banner of Max Linder Productions. He rented a house right around the corner from Chaplin and developed a close relationship with him. According to Grace Kingsley, 'Linder and Chaplin are great pals, it seems, and discuss their plans and the gags for their pictures as freely as though they didn't belong to the same fraternity.'[5] This relationship lasted throughout Linder's second stay in the States, which ended in summer 1922. They were often reported together attending film premieres and going out to dinner. One such evening at Linder's house, Chaplin brought along a bird as a gift, which sang, danced and preened itself: 'When Linder started to feed and water the bird, he found that it was a mechanical toy.'[6]

There was no shooting then from 20 February through 9 March. On 10 March, retakes were shot of Jackie on the street set. The next day, Tom Wilson as the policeman was filmed at a broken glass window, and this was repeated in close up the following day, as was a close up of Jackie standing at a door. Tests were shot at night of the heaven scene, so by this date, 12 March, Chaplin had come up with this heaven scene add-on, another dream sequence, either to bring his film to six reels, to utilize Lillita McMurray in the film (Lita Grey, his future wife) or perhaps for some other unknown reason. On the

13 and 15 March, however, he did not jump right into the heaven scene as expected, but returned to the attic set for retakes. Then on 17 March, the note in the production report read 'First D guns,' meaning that some fifty-plus First National exhibitors and officers descended on the Chaplin studios for the day, to see what, if anything, Chaplin was actually accomplishing there. Photos were shot and film was taken during the visit, showing clear evidence that Chaplin was prepared in advance for it, for he showed off his youngsters (Jackie even did his shimmy for the group) and everyone seemed to go home happy – although dark days were to come regarding Chaplin-First National relations. For now, the great comedian had bought himself some time.

That effort must have taken the wind out of him, because no more shooting took place from 18 March until the day after Chaplin's birthday on 16 April. In between filming Chaplin was getting in a bit of trouble and causing himself some embarrassment. Although many versions of this evening exist, the one reported by the *Los Angeles Times* the following day by the Alexandria Hotel management has the most credibility. After Mildred's announcement on 18 March that she was considering divorce, the rumor mill in Hollywood created a narrative that Chaplin was sending his colleagues and friends to her at every opportunity to get her to either reconsider, or to agree to accept a small settlement, $5,000 in one report and $25,000 in another. Her new producer, the as-yet unpowerful Louis B. Mayer, supposedly made it known that he strongly objected to this sort of treatment of his star and verbally denigrated Chaplin for the behavior. Fast forward to the night of 7 April 1920. Chaplin was seated at the Alexandria Hotel at a table with Marshall Neilan, Agnes Ayres, Jack Pickford and others. Louis B. Mayer was a member of a party of twelve at Anita Stewart's, one of his client's, table. At some point in the evening, a note was delivered to Chaplin, which he read and stepped out into the lobby. Mayer received a similar note and did the same. As Mayer approached Chaplin, he heard the diminutive star say to him, 'take off your glasses,' which the much larger man did. Chaplin then landed a right hook to Mayer's jaw, which didn't faze the larger man whose immediate response was a bash on Chaplin's nose, under the weight of which Chaplin fell. As he went down, Mayer grabbed him by the nose, leaving some visible marks.[7]

The Alexandria staff broke up the fight and Jack Pickford took charge of Chaplin, sending him home in the Pickford car. Mayer returned to his table. Two factors are of particular interest here: first, J.D. Williams, First National boss and the person Chaplin usually had to deal with directly regarding his contract, was at the Stewart table; when interviewed, Mayer claimed that Williams was with him when Chaplin threw his punch. Second, Rollie Totheroh later claimed that Jack Pickford had sent those two notes to the men as a joke.[8] That little, uncharacteristic, burst of violence on the part of Chaplin encapsulates in a few brief moments the months and years of creative frustration he must have felt at the hands of First National – a feeling now tied to Mildred, the woman from whom he was estranged. First National had bought and paid for her and so she could no longer be trusted; confronted with the rotund, glistening, sycophantic Mayer, Chaplin had lashed out in order to feel some sense of relief at last. Unfortunately, he only made himself look more sad and silly. The following day, only Mayer could be found for comment, and he made assurance that no warrant would be sworn out for Chaplin's arrest. He apologized for the public nature of the confrontation, saying 'I feel very sorry the thing took place where it did, and I feel that I owe an apology to the public and the management of the hotel for the occurrence and my unintentional part in it.'[9] Even Chaplin's lawyer, Arthur Wright, wasn't able to contact his client for a response.

In some sense, this episode was not quite over. Chaplin sent a cable on 9 April to his brother in New York which read, 'Impending trouble STOP Will ship negative to you for safety. Wire advice immediately.'[10] Obviously, his shenanigans at the Alexandria had led to a deep paranoia that Mildred would now proceed with the divorce and that meant she would try to take half of everything he owned. His first worries then focused on the film in production and this cable suggested he was already harboring the idea of transporting it somewhere outside of Los Angeles for safety. About a week later, another cable suggested that the brothers had decided to, for now, place the Chaplin Studios and Charlie Chaplin Film Company under new ownership, namely Syd's, also in an attempt to keep it from being attached by Mildred's lawyers. Syd took over ownership of the two on 15 April,[11] so Charlie celebrated his 30th birthday sans studio or film company. His uncompleted film, however, was still in danger.

Finally, back at the studio on 17 April, the shot was produced of what appears to be Christ carrying his cross on Calvary, but was actually shot on Eagle Rock. The scene with Edna approaching the 'charity hospital' was shot at Occidental College on 21 and 22 April, with Beulah Bain, Purviance's stand-in, being used in her place. Three days of retakes were shot in the attic set on 30 April, 1 May, and 3 May, followed by tests of angel women on 6 May, but no other shooting was accomplished until 14 May, when Chaplin was concentrating on the flophouse set to which Jackie and Charlie flee after being chased from their flat by the welfare officers. Shooting on this set continued until 28 May, when it was expanded to the street (some location shooting was done as well at Universal City), and then the heaven set filming was begun in earnest on 30 May, but with stops and starts in the filming from then on. Chaplin had once again been forced to ask First National for an extension of time to complete his eight required films, and a letter he received from Harry Schwalbe on 20 May illustrates that he successfully received such permission:

we wish to advise you that at this time, as you know, there are four of said photoplays remaining undelivered, and that we are of the same desire and intent as expressed to you in our letter of 5 March 1919, not to take advantage or to stand upon any question of time of delivery, on the pictures, but on the contrary are willing to grant, and do hereby grant, any further and additional reasonable extensions of time in addition to those granted in our letter of 5 March 1919 for the delivery of said photoplays remaining undelivered.[12]

Film was shot on the heaven set 1 June, but not again until the 9 and then steadily until the 16, with the 'lunch wagon bus[iness]' shot on 10 June. After a break then of three days, shooting resumed on this set on the 22 June and continued until the 4 July holiday, with just a couple of days off, then picked back up until 14 July, when Chaplin was out with a hurt finger and the 15th, when Jackie went home sick. Filming picked up again the following day, with the weather described as 'warm and earthquaky.' Filming on the heaven set was completed on 22 July with the swan dance. This scene, for many, is somewhat controversial, because it seems a bit 'added on.' Grace Kingsley, having been permitted a visit to the set during the filming of this scene, had an interesting take on it once she wrote a review for the film seven months later:

In his latest picture, Charlie Chaplin is revealed as the [J.M.] Barrie[13] of the slum photodrama. *The Kid* is Barrie vulgarized but superbly whimsical, vital, robust.

Not even Barrie's slavey heroine's conception of a court ball equals in imagination, humor or whimsicality Chaplin's conception of heaven.

As the poor roustabout, he falls asleep after the mad search for his kidnapped foster-son, and dreams of celestial life. Such delicious, harmless fun, too. Nobody could possibly take offense. Even when Sin gets in, and there's a rough-house among the angels, who can feel aught but laughter when the feathers fly? And who that has lost a pet won't sympathize with the small boy meeting his winged pup?

Not that there is the slightest suggestion of the conscious imitation of Barrie's methods. It is only that, in Chaplin's humor as well as in his drama, there is the same whimsicality, the same striking at vital human truths with the gleaming sword of fun.[14]

Thinking of Jackie as one of Barrie's lost boys or even Charlie and Jackie as two of those boys, their playground the slum streets of the city, their escape from this world the heaven of their dreamscapes certainly changes the usual reading of the scene and makes it less solemn – that reading being that Charlie believes that Jackie has died and that he can only dream of them together again in heaven.

The final scenes of the film took up the last week of the month: 23–26 July on the interior of the police station, 28 July on an exterior shot in Chinatown, and finally, 30 July on the exterior of Edna's house, shot on location at Wilshire and Wilshire Place.[15] Cutting began 31 July and continued until about 20 August; Mildred had filed for divorce on 3 August and Chaplin feared that the film might be seized as one of his financial assets, so Chaplin and company departed to Salt Lake City, Utah, with the film on 5 August. Mildred's divorce complaint was filed on the grounds of extreme mental cruelty and bodily injury. In addition:

Mrs Chaplin also asks that her husband be restrained from disposing of his interest in certain motion picture films and that he be required to account to the court for sums received by him on her account during their married life, and that if such sums are insufficient to enable her to live in her present station of life to make such order as the court deems equitable and just.[16]

Because the entire complaint was published in the press in detail and Mildred was besieged by reporters thereafter, a statement was issued two days later that confirmed the filing, because her ambiguous response to these reporters had created some doubt. Chaplin filed no countercomplaint. He was too busy trying to get out of town.

The best account of this hasty departure is provided by Chaplin's loyal cameraman, Rollie Totheroh in a 1972 interview. At 3.00 am on 5 August, Totheroh was awakened to find Chaplin Studios manager Alf Reeves at his door:

> He said, 'Rollie, come on. We have to get out of town. Use a fictional name.' I asked him if I could take my assistant, Jack Wilson, along with me and he said yes. 'But get right over to the studio and get ahold of the carpenter and have everything crated.' I knew trouble was brewing. We didn't know where we were going but we had to get ahold of Tom Harrington, who was supposed to have the tickets. So Jack and I went down to the Santa Fe depot after we got all the film of *The Kid* packed in coffee tins, in two-hundred-foot rolls, loose all the way packed solid on top; there were about twelve cases of it, all in negative. And Charlie was at the depot. He had his black glasses on, but he had taken off his disguise. He was sitting at the table just about to be waited on and this little kid sitting at the table across the way said, 'Charlie Chaplin! Charlie Chaplin!' So, we had to beat it out of there.[17]

So, Chaplin, Rollie Totheroh and Jack Wilson, his two cameramen and Tom Harrington, his valet, arrived in Salt Lake City on Saturday afternoon, 7 August, and took up residence at the Hotel Utah, where the actor registered as 'Charles Spencer.' It took the press a mere twenty-four hours to find and corner him, with the first interviews appearing the next day in which Chaplin defended his departure from Los Angeles, his stay in Salt Lake City and even his false name. Chaplin, in green silk pajamas as it was late in the evening, answered the door to the journalist himself, who later wrote that 'everything about Mr Chaplin's room at the hotel was immaculate today,'[18] suggesting that either he expected to see cans of film strewn about or that Chaplin had planned for such intrusions and stashed the film in another room. According to one report, 'the titles and sub-heads are not yet written. It has to be cut in places and much remolding of minor original ideas will take place before it is finally called completed.'[19] However, it is clear from a close reading of Totheroh's accounting of the trip that little to no cutting took place in Salt Lake City, contrary to the way it has been mythologized since that time.

As the media was soon to discover, Chaplin had consulted counsel before his flight to determine a place where he and his film would be safe from the Los Angeles process servers who sought to seize *The Kid* as part of the Mildred Harris divorce suit, and Utah was the place. He could remain there safely, seemingly as long as he liked. Chaplin suggested to the press that his film up to this point had cost $300,000 plus $5,000 per week to keep the studio and its staff up and running[20] (with the film taking two years[21]), so it was this investment that he was trying to protect. Meanwhile, Mildred had the date of the divorce complaint moved back to 16 August, in order to give the process servers more time to find her husband. Brother Syd was reported to be in town 13 August to help out,[22] but the group's tenure in Salt Lake City was about to end, as they were asked to leave about a week later, probably because there was no appropriate film laboratory in the city, so Chaplin and company's occupation there had to be suspect. They departed the city for New York on 23 August, having to transfer trains and experience a layover in Chicago on the way. Along with the precious twelve cases of film, Chaplin was in constant contact with what Totheroh deemed 'the black bag':

> We got to Chicago and had a wait-over. We transferred over and went over before the train came in. We stood in a circle, all of these people milling around. He said, 'Put that bag between your legs, Rollie. Don's let anybody near it.' I knew he had valuables in it, but he had everything he had in there – all these cash bonds

and everything else. One man came walking by and stood near us just looking at us. Charlie gave him this dirty look and told him to beat it. And the guy gave him a look and wondered what the devil he was doing. Charlie said, 'Keep away from this here. Keep away!'[23]

Once in New York, Chaplin went to see Nathan Burkan and Totheroh and Wilson were charged with finding an appropriately discreet film laboratory. Luckily, Wilson was acquainted with David Horsley of the former Centaur Studios, located at 900 Broadway in Bayonne, New Jersey.[24] Once contacted, Horsley readily gave his permission and the two set about transporting the film across the river from New York to New Jersey in what turned out to be a very dangerous journey, according to Totheroh:

> when we got the truck that had our film on it, it was the busy time of the day, and we were crossing the river going over to New Jersey. I could smell the fumes from the nitrate but I didn't realize what it was. I had a hunch that the vibrations could raise hell with us. Anyhow, when I opened a lot of tins – especially the ones at the bottom of the tins – they were just ready to explode. Supposing they would have exploded on the ferry-boats; I had them marked 'Machine Tools'![25]

Upon arrival at last, the two attached a sign to the lab that read 'Blue Moon Film Company,' so that the whole thing appeared legitimate and began a 24/7 work schedule with very few breaks. Instead of Salt Lake City then, *The Kid* was born into its final form in Bayonne, New Jersey. Word of the operation spread, and the criminal element came calling one night in particular:

> One night I came outside to get a breath of fresh air and there were two guys standing out there, Italian-looking guys. They

said, 'You have Chaplin's film here, we know that. You can make yourself $30,000. All you have to do is keep the vault unlocked and we'll take care of the rest of it.' So I told them that all we had there was work-print. I said, 'We don't have the negative, that stuff is probably in the vaults in New York.' After that, of course, we got a couple of guards to stand watch.[26]

It was reported that Chaplin had been trying to sell the film out from under First National in the meantime and, of course, First National soon found this out and began publishing full page ads warning possible buyers against such a purchase. Each was titled 'Regarding Charles Chaplin and "The Kid"' and dated 28 August 1920. It detailed the points of Chaplin's contract with First National and warned that 'Charles Chaplin has no right or authority to produce motion pictures for any person, firm or corporation or to sell any motion pictures produced by him to any person, firm or corporation other than the said First National Exhibitors' Circuit, Inc.'[27] In fact, they based their concern on an interview Chaplin gave in Salt Lake City[28] in which he claimed he would stay in that state until 'the picture is sold' and had several interested parties there in Salt Lake at the time[29] In fact, the chronology of Chaplin's finalizing a deal with First National, i.e., achieving a reasonable change to his contract in regards to remuneration, is confusing.

Chaplin and company left Salt Lake City on 23 August and had to transfer trains in Chicago. How long this delay was is not certain, but since Totheroh remembered only that they waited at the station standing in a circle around the precious luggage, it would seem that the layover was not that long. This would put the group in New York City then no later than 26 August. This then gives Totheroh and Wilson eight days to cut the film and get a work print ready to show to the First National folks, have them initially balk at and then cave into Chaplin's demands by 3 September, when Charlie sends Syd a cryptic telegram back to Salt Lake City with the details of what ends up being the final deal: $800,000 with $400,000 cash on delivery (or thereabouts) and the rest paid upon delivery of the final three films owed for the contract. As Chaplin writes to Syd in the cable (addressed to S. Gilbert from M. Gilbert, 3 September 1920), this deal was achieved over three days of sessions.[30] It also states that First National would not handle it as a special, but by early 1921, they had changed their mind on this, because it becomes part of 'The Big Five' – five special films to be released at the same time in February 1921. Another confusing piece of evidence regarding the chronology of this deal is an article in *Wid's Daily*, dated 11 September 1920,[31] that claims Chaplin had just arrived in New York 8 September and was in the midst of negotiations with First National at that time. Finally, the actual contract addendum that detailed this deal, was not signed until 3 December 1920.

Meanwhile, as of 27 August, Mildred had turned down Chaplin's offer to her of a flat $125,000 ($25,000 or $45,000 in other reports), saying to the press that he was worth at least $1 million and she was seeking half of that, as well as half the value of *The Kid*.[32] By 13 September, Mildred was broadcasting the claim that she would not give Chaplin a divorce after all, but that she intended to work towards a financial settlement, knowing now, through her lawyers, that he was worth $3 million dollars and that some of his property had been transferred over into Syd's name.[33] Two days later, Mildred decided to settle for only half the value of *The Kid* and had her lawyers put a lien on it at that point.[34] The very next day, Chaplin announced to the press that he would be leaving for England soon for an indefinite period, obviously with some thought of taking his film with him, although this wasn't mentioned. This announcement seemed to be bolstered by the report that Carter de Haven had successfully rented the Chaplin studios from Syd for six months as of 8 October, for the sum of $1,250 per week.[35] However, a mere two days later, the media reported that Chaplin would be returning to Hollywood as soon as the Mildred Harris divorce had been settled, i.e., there would be no trip to England at this time. As for the de Haven studio rental, Chaplin stated that the studio was indeed large enough to accommodate two productions at once and that there would be no problem sharing the property with Mr de Haven for the six-month lease.[36] Perhaps one positive effect of all the waffling on Mildred's part was that the public began to turn on her and toward Chaplin: 'Our sympathy in the Chaplin divorce case is gradually shifting over on Charlie's side. If Mildred Harris Chaplin talked to Charlie as much as she does to the newspaper reporters, we don't blame him for leaving her.'[37]

The 6 November, Mildred announced that she would finally consent to dropping the 'Chaplin' from her name, as Charlie had been asking her to do.[38] This was actually a signal, for on 13 November the day dawned on the end of the Chaplin/Harris marriage. The end came quickly and unexpectedly for all concerned. Mildred received a cable from Louis B. Mayer to get herself to New York, where a Judge York had been secured to try the case in Probate court immediately. Chaplin himself was not present, but his interests were presented and protected by Arthur Wright. Mildred was accompanied only by her mother. Married at 17, she was divorced and had lost a baby by 19. Her financial settlement was $200,000.[39] Chaplin emerged from hiding on 15 November to sign the divorce papers in the office of W.I. Gilbert. He would be back in Hollywood in time for Christmas.

But before he could return home, Chaplin had a little business to conduct. His faithful cameramen Rollie Totheroh and Jack Wilson had completed a work print of *The Kid* in the New Jersey lab and Chaplin wanted to screen it for the First National bosses while he was in town, because he wanted to renegotiate his contract to include this six-reeler, and have it treated differently from the other films. Without a renegotiation, he would get about $405,000. With it, he hoped to get at least $1 million. This preview was supposed to provide direct evidence to First National as to why the film was worth more money to Chaplin than the original contract called for. The screening had to have taken place sometime between 12 November, the date Chaplin's divorce was finalized and 3 December, when the contract addendum was signed. However, instead of singing Chaplin's praises during and after the screening, the bosses chose to spend the screening ridiculing him. Chaplin commented later to his cameraman, 'You know that picture we made, Rollie? With the out-takes from all the others? Let's splice that together and give it to them.'[40] But First National very soon decided in Chaplin's favor. The contract addendum signed 3 December called for $800,000 for this particular film, with $200,000 paid on delivery, $200,000 thirty days after delivery, then $133,333 with delivery of each of the three remaining films owed on the contract.[41] Chaplin did not hand the finished film over to First National's Sol Lesser until 30 December 1920.

January was spent in speculation as to when the film would be released and whether it would be released as a special or as one of the eight required for Chaplin's contract. Although several articles[42] seem to assert that *The Kid* was finally deemed a special and would be released as part of 'The Big Five' films, which included *Passion* with Pola Negri, *Man-Woman-Marriage* with Dorothy Phillips, *The Oath*, a Raoul Walsh production and *Sowing the Wind* with Anita Stewart, in reality, the film was counted as one of the eight, leaving Chaplin only three films to produce in order to complete his contract. Rank and file First National Exhibitors previewed the film on 5 February 1921, and then the film was finally released the next day.

After the struggles involved in producing *Sunnyside* and *A Day's Pleasure*, Chaplin must have been heartened by the reception of his first feature, *The Kid*, for it surpassed both of his two other successful First National productions, *A Dog's Life* and *Shoulder Arms*. It broke all records at the Strand in New York, where it played to 125,000 people in the first week, with extra morning and midnight performances instated to try to accommodate the crowds.[43] Chicago welcomed vast crowds who waited in line in the cold to see the film at the Randolph Theater there. Its *Herald-Examiner* for 17 January presented a review that was highly laudatory. It began, 'Yesterday morning about 9 all

the film comedians who have been taking Chaplin's place took their
hats in their hands and eased themselves out the back way.' This critic
unabashedly claimed that this picture 'settles once and for all the
question of whom is the greatest theatrical artist in the world.' He
asserted that:

> Chaplin in it does some of the lowest of low comedy, at which
> you rock and writhe, but he also does some of the finest, most
> delicately shaded acting you ever saw anywhere, and for every
> slapstick furor in it there is a classic, exquisite scene which only
> the greatest of painters will fully appreciate.[44]

Similar sentiments were echoed by many other critics in New York
and throughout the country. The *New York Morning Telegraph* noted
that, 'It is the only picture of its kind ever made. A mixture of knock-
out comedy, pathos, and whimsical humor, it takes its place with the
classics of the screen.' The *New York Globe* offered that 'Chaplin gives
you something that brings a lump to the throat while you are roaring
with laughter.'[45] The *Los Angeles Times*'s Grace Kingsley likened
the film to 'a drink of water after a day's hot thirst.' She admitted
it was something new in form, but 'so simple that like most great
achievements, one wonders why it wasn't done before.' She suggested
'it has all the old melodramatic material, but so jazzed up with fun
and with its drama so simply and humanly played, that it almost fools
you into believing it is like life. In this, Chaplin's art is seen.'[46] Because
cinemagoers had not seen Chaplin for a year, most were also calling
the film his successful comeback as well.

This success did not buy him any leniency or understanding from
First National, however. He still owed them three films and would
be held to that agreement. Back in Hollywood, Chaplin was already
working on Production No. 6. He would not spend an entire year on
another First National film, but his final three productions would
take him well into the year 1923 anyway.

Chapter 6

Back to Work in Hollywood:
Filming *The Idle Class*

Referring to the Chaplin that returned to Hollywood after his several-months-long ordeal in New York as a 'grass-widower,' a now archaic term that once labeled a man who, without a wife, would have to do all of the domestic duties of the household himself, reporters all noted that he looked fit, refreshed and well-decked-out in new clothes, even carrying a cane. Chaplin arrived back in Hollywood at 8.00 pm on 9 December and shied away from all questions about his now former marriage, choosing instead to concentrate on the imminent release of his new film *The Kid*.[1] About a week later, he entertained the press at the studio, suggesting he was back to work on the three short comedies still required, which would be nothing like *The Kid*, but 'for laughing purposes only.' Once this obligation was completed, he offered that he would be able to carry out some big things he had been contemplating for some time.[2] In reality, Chaplin was not back at the studio to begin on the next production, initially titled *Home Again*, until 29 January 1921 and then didn't actually begin shooting until 15 February, for the first two weeks were taken up with talking story, finding locations, casting, testing actors and fitting costumes.

Perhaps the semi-late start was due to a bit of turmoil over at United Artists, championed by Doug Fairbanks[3] and Mary Pickford – a merger between UA and Associated Producers about 7 January. Grace Kingsley reported that the merger was a very important one that had been contemplated for a long time, 'but certain members of both organizations were uncertain regarding the benefits to be derived, one of these dissenters being Charlie Chaplin, but Chaplin has now been completely won over.'[4] The new combine would include, in addition to the founding four, Thomas Ince, Allan Dwan, Mack Sennett, Marshall Neilan, Maurice Tourneur, and George Loane Tucker. As important as this merger seemed to be at the time, indeed it never occurred, for United Artists president Hiram Abrams had announced by 18 January that the deal was off.[5] Associated Producers would align with First National instead later that year.

From the reports, it appears that Carlyle Robinson, who had been the Chaplin Studios' publicity director during the Liberty Loan tour and had departed when he was called into service, was now back in its employ and Edward A. Biby, who had occupied the publicity director position since that time, was gone. The child from the heaven scene in *The Kid*, Lillita McMurray (destined to become the second Mrs Chaplin) was listed now as 'Lolita Parker' on the rolls for this production from the first day of filming to the last, along with her mother Mrs Parker and her teacher. Now a teenager, the girl and her mother can be seen only as Edna's character's domestic help in certain scenes, suggesting that Chaplin possibly already had some ulterior motive for keeping her near him. Chaplin directed only on 15 February and from the list of cast members, it appears he began at the beginning, with the wealthy arriving at the train station. There were even three porters in the cast whose role is merely 'atmosphere.' This scene took two days and was filmed at the Santa Fe Depot in Los Angeles. Nothing was shot on 17 February due to rain, and then Chaplin shot one more day with himself, Edna, Lita, and her mother, most likely being transported from the station to their residence. By 23 February, with just a few days of filming having been completed and two days shut down for rain, Chaplin was cutting the film together to see what he had. No work was done between 24 and 28 February due to new sets being prepared. Chaplin stepped on a large nail on an indoor stage at the studios on 28 February, crawled in agony to his dressing room and was treated by Dr. Tilman McLaughlin,[6] who suggested he give the foot some time to heal to avoid an infection; this resulted in five days off from 1 to 5 March. This production was getting started very slowly indeed.

About this time, the First National Exhibitors' Circuit system of distributing films to theaters was coming under some scrutiny by its member theaters. In essence, the theater owners of New York state, through the body of the New York Chamber of Commerce, recommended to their members officially that they comply with the original tenets of the contract with First National regarding distribution of Chaplin's *The Kid* and strongly request that First National Exhibitors' Circuit do the same. First National replied that this mandate was 'an insult to any exhibitor's sense of square dealing and fair play,' adding that theaters across the country were 'cheerfully' waiving their contracts and agreeing to the new prices necessitated by the renegotiation of Chaplin's contract for the film and by First National's agreeing to make the film a 'special,' and therefore, not one of the eight films with its price guaranteed by the original contract:

Associated First National Pictures is not asking the individual exhibitor to do anything which it has not been willing to do itself, as shown by the manner its franchise holders have agreed to increased rentals on 'The Kid.' It is merely asking the exhibitor to observe the same spirit of fairness and justice regarding the rental price of the picture that its Purchasing Committee exercised when obtaining the production for the benefit of its franchise and sub-franchise holders.[7]

In other words, the original contract expected the Chaplin product to consist only of short comedies two reels in length. *The Kid*, at six reels, simply could not be covered by this original contract in a manner that was fair to Chaplin, to First National and to its exhibitors as well. But this was not to be the end of an undertow of bad feelings between the First National bosses and their franchisees. It only loosened the threads on what was already an unstable package that would continue to come loose over the course of 1921 and beyond.

On 3 March 1921, the resolution finally came to the problem of bringing Charlie and Syd's mother Hannah Chaplin to the United States, a task that Syd especially had been trying to make happen since 1916, when her last caretaker, aunt Kate Mowbray, died in June of that year. World War I made it impossible for the brothers to bring her over at that point in time, so Syd did his best to arrange for her care through cousin Aubrey Chaplin, who, because he had his own aspirations about moving to California and working for Charlie at some point,[8] bent over backwards in providing as much assistance to the brothers as graciously as possible, which wasn't always easy. On 30 November 1918, Peckham House, Hannah's residence at the time, received notice of her imminent departure for the States from Syd, who had waited only for the Treaty of Versailles to be signed before making such a move. Charlie, experiencing some creative challenges, halted the procedure with a note to Syd that read, 'Second thoughts. Consider will be best mother will remain in England. Some good seaside resort. Afraid presence here might depress and effect my work.'[9] By March 1921 and with the labor of *The Kid* behind him, Charlie didn't have much to say about putting the trip off further, so Syd went ahead.

Aubrey Chaplin and his wife prepared Hannah for her voyage on the British side and Tom Harrington was elected to be her chaperone from the American side. Harrington and Mrs Chaplin took the S.S. *Celtic* out of Liverpool on 16 March, landing in New York on 26 March, where Hannah supposedly identified her inspector at Customs and Immigration as Jesus Christ, in what is now considered an apocryphal ejaculation. The two then made it to Hollywood by 3 April and Mrs Chaplin was installed at Chaplin's residence on Temple Hill Drive[10] in the interim while a suitable residence was found for her. The location of her residence was then kept secret, for obvious reasons, but she was indulged and well-cared for until her death on 28 August in 1928, despite the U.S. government's several attempts to have her deported.[11] While she had round-the-clock caretakers, the Chaplin studios' wives, such as Mrs Amy Reeves, Wyn Ritchie (widow of Billie Ritchie), Minnie Chaplin and others were regular visitors. Chaplin himself visited sparingly and was often dismayed to find that his mother knew nothing of his fame and current financial standing, or even of how he made his living.

Home Again resumed filming on 7 March through to 11 March with Chaplin, Henry Bergman and an actor named Rex Storey engaged in hijinks on the golf course at the Pasadena Golf Club,[12] which is one of the main locations of the film. J.D. Williams popped into town this week as well and, of course, paid a visit to the Chaplin Studios, but without the huge group of exhibitors this time. The two's initial conversation was reported as simply: Chaplin to Williams: 'Well, J.D.?' Williams to Chaplin: 'Wonderful, Charlie. Simply wonderful.'[13] And thus was their exchange on *The Kid*. From this, one would think that all was well again between First National and its recalcitrant star, but the peace was short-lived. Williams was in town for about ten days visiting with each of his stars to check up on their latest productions. He owned to one reporter that Chaplin's film took the honors among the First National stars for the early part of the year but thought that some other film and its stars might well take over those honors later in the year – all in the name of keeping a healthy competition going between his many stars and their production companies.[14]

Chaplin was cutting again on 12 and 14 March to see what he had (it was raining those days anyway). On the 15 and 16 March, Chaplin was filming only with Purviance, 17 March with John Rand and a goat, 19 March with Rand and a young couple, 21 March with Purviance and the horse – another horse and a mule were used, this being the daydream sequence in which Charlie imagines himself saving Edna from a runaway horse. Filming stopped on 24 March due to waiting for the interior sets to be finished, then three days were taken off for a location trip, then 29 March was off again waiting for the interior sets. Filming picked up, though, the next day for two days. The 1 and 2 April were off due to waiting for sets and 3 April was spent rehearsing. From 5 to 7 April filming resumed with Loyal Underwood, Al Garcia, Henry Bergman, and a dog, which may have been the cut scenes in the bowling alley with Chaplin as the rich husband; Chaplin stopped to cut on 8 through 13 April. About this time, reports began to appear linking Chaplin with 17-year-old Broadway actress May Collins, who had recently moved to Hollywood, after meeting Chaplin in New York when he was there in the Fall of 1920. This first article appeared 7 April and the two were already talking marriage.[15] Collins had a lengthy resumé for one so young, which probably impressed Chaplin. In the second week of April she was about to make her theatrical debut in Los Angeles at the Little Theatre in McHugh's *True to Form*[16] and Chaplin was there on opening night to wish her well. By the end of April, she already had a contract with Universal, her first film project being *The Shark Master* with Frank Mayo.[17] But by May, the reports had fizzled out and Chaplin was reported as trying out some new dance steps at the recently opened Ambassador Hotel with Claire Windsor. He was obviously not about to get tied down again so soon and would be linked to several females in the next few years.

Back on the *Idle Class* production, 14 and 15 April they waited for sets again and 16 April they prepared the story, indicating that perhaps the bowling set hadn't worked out. It's worth noting that this is the first year that Chaplin's birthday is mentioned in the paper, indicating, perhaps, that *The Kid* has placed him at a level of celebrity that he hadn't occupied before. He celebrated with Pickford and Fairbanks at Pickfair, the Fairbanks' estate, along with a few other film friends.[18] Filming resumed between 18 and 21 April, again with Mack Swain, Al Garcia, and Henry Bergman and one news report offered that more than 2,000 people blocked traffic, watching the famous comedian perform this day.[19] Swain would be Chaplin's heavy in this film at 6ft 4in in height and weighing 250 pounds.[20] The two hadn't worked together since the Keystone days.

The 22 April was spent hunting for locations, and 25 and 26 April were spent cutting the picture again. Filming resumed 27 April again with Swain, Garcia and Bergman, with Chaplin only on 28 April and with Purviance, the Parkers (Lita and her mother) and Harry Maynard on 29 April. Also on the 29 April, the law firm of King and Schulder of Salt Lake City were forced to sue Chaplin for $25,000, the amount of money he owed them for legal services rendered to him during his flight from Los Angeles away from Mildred Harris's divorce claim.[21] The firm had trouble serving the actor with a subpoena, but the case finally came to federal court presided over by Judge Page Morris in late April 1922. Chaplin, who was represented by his brother Syd (with Tom Harrington in tow), claimed that the services rendered had not been worth more than $500. The plaintiff did admit during testimony that their original bill had been for only $10,000. After closing arguments on Tuesday 2 May, the jury was instructed to decide the value of service provided to Chaplin by King and Schulder and place the 'verdict' in a sealed envelope to be read in court the following morning.[22] When the verdict was read on 3 May, the Salt Lake law firm was awarded a $4,000 fee from Chaplin, exactly $500 more than the actor had offered the firm to settle the matter out of court. Neither party would appeal the decision.[23]

Then on 30 April more cutting was done and new sets were prepared. Waiting for sets continued until 4 May, when filming resumed the next day with Chaplin, six actresses and an actor, Harald Kent, on what was probably the scene in which the rich husband finds himself in a phone booth or box in his hotel without his pants and must find a way to escape. Chaplin was badly burned filming this sequence. As one report indicated, he tripped over the blow torch used in the scene and his clothing immediately caught fire. Chaplin's legs were particularly burned before the blaze could be extinguished with blankets, but luckily he had donned asbestos undergarments before filming, or his injuries would have been worse.[24] Between 5 and 8 May filming was complicated by rain, but shooting continued on 9 and 10 May, again with Purviance, the Parkers, and Harry Maynard, and then with Maynard only on 11 May. Harry Maynard had actually been hired by Chaplin as his art director,[25] but it seems that since he had some experience acting, he was employed in that capacity as well here. More cutting was done on 13 May. It is clear from the reports that scenes in which Chaplin as the rich husband returns to his wife's apartments, a scene that included the Parkers, as well as Edna Purviance, were shot during this run of filming. Between 16 and 18 May they waited for sets, 19 May for costumes and 20 and 21 May for the rain.

Filming resumed on 23 May and continued unabated until 9 June when Chaplin stayed home sick until 15 June. It turns out that he had come down with the flu, as had many in Hollywood, including Mary Pickford and Nazimova.[26] But that wasn't all that was going on with Chaplin at this time. A man named Henry Baker, a pressman from Tacoma, Washington, sent a death threat to Chaplin – one so serious that the star decided to report it, which resulted in the man's arrest. Baker told Chaplin in the letter that he needed to send him $30,000 or lose his life, and then provided his name and address, so that the funds could be sent. The really troubling part for Chaplin was Baker's sign-off of 'Comet cause.'[27] Although the meaning of this was unclear, a dangerous comet, Winnecke's, was in the Earth's vicinity at the time and could have been some sort of additional cryptic threat on Baker's part. [28]

Some cutting was also done on this day. Al Garcia, new to the Chaplin stable and probably introduced to him by Syd, for whom he worked on the ill-fated *King, Queen, Joker* in 1919, was reported working 25 May only with Chaplin, so this was probably the scene on the bench taken at the park across the street from the Beverly Hills Hotel, the only scene in which Garcia is recognizable, although he is listed as part of the fancy dress ball scene and several other scenes as well.[29] Chaplin was shot with E.C. Kolkum alone on 30 May and with both Kolkum and Mack Swain on the 31st. The reports for 6 and 7 June contain the most extras and all cast members are listed as 'working,' so this was most likely the filming of the fancy dress ball scenes.

Chaplin was ill again on 16 June, cutting on 17 and 18 and talking story on the 19th. It wasn't until about this date that the press was given some idea of what the story would be about, and reports appeared that Chaplin would be playing dual roles in the film.[30] Filming then continued until completed on 25 June 1921, with Mack Swain and John Rand sharing the scene with Chaplin on those final days, suggesting he filmed more antics on the golf course then.[31] The title *The Idle Class* is written in pencil at the top of the report for 24 June for the first time, but it wasn't announced to the press until 15 July.[32] The press had originally been given the title *Vanity Fair*, instead of *Home Again* for the picture. The finished film was delivered to First National's John McGormick by Alf Reeves on 16 August 1921, but was not released to theaters until 25 September 1921, about the halfway point in his homecoming trip to England.

When they did arrive, the notices and reviews of the film were mostly positive – truly a feat considering that this was the first film after *The Kid*. In San Francisco, 'a general stampede of determined humanity awaited the opening of the doors at 10.15 am and fairly stormed the theater unceasingly until long after the box office had closed for the night, incidentally, shattering all previous attendance records at the Strand. After they got inside, Charlie simply knocked "em dead.'[33] In Los Angeles, it was reported that '75,000 Angelenos have taken a new lease on life. At least that is the estimated number who saw Charlie Chaplin's latest, *The Idle Class*, at the Kinema Theatre last week,'[34] The very next day however, T.J. Tally's theater was reportedly *not* drawing crowds equal to either *The Kid* or even *Shoulder Arms*.[35] Of course, old stalwart Chaplin backers like Grace Kingsley continued to see in each new film the brilliance that could only be Chaplin's: '*The Idle Class* is as freshly original, as full of brilliant touches, as adroitly put over as only a man who has worked as long and as faithfully and as cleverly as Charlie Chaplin could make it.'[36] Heywood Broun, noted New York journalist and member of the Algonquin Round Table there, celebrated his move to the *New York World* from the *New York Tribune* in 1921 with a laudatory review of Chaplin and his film, one which was soon used on full-page ads of the film in the industry rags: 'If we may begin to lay bets in an effort to pick some particular man of our generation who will later on be called a genius, we should like to back Chaplin.'[37]

Back in August, *Variety* had reported that Chaplin had asked First National for more money for this picture. This request meant that 'an increase on the picture will undoubtedly be passed along to the exhibitors in increased rentals on the production. The outstanding contracts with exhibitors on the Chaplin releases are to be called in and new contracts issued.'[38] In fact, Chaplin was able to negotiate a new contract for *The Idle Class*, one with four main points that differed from the original contract he signed in June 1917. This new contract, signed after his return from Europe on 31 October 1921, stipulated that 1) Chaplin was now to receive 35 per cent of the entire total gross receipts of everything earned over $250,000 from whatever source, 2) he was now to receive each and every exhibitor booking contract for approval, 3) he was now to receive an itemized statement on the fifteenth of each month after the release of a photoplay showing all business reported to First National in the preceding month, and 4) he was now to be paid for *The Idle Class* an agreed upon amount *in addition* to moneys accruing to him 'on account of such photoplay under the agreement between First National and Chaplin dated June 19, 1917' (the date of the original contract).[39] This may have led to a record 120 prints of the film being released in the New York territory alone, due to an increase in the length of film runs. In other words, the film was playing in several New York houses at the same time. After the huge success of *The Kid*, First National originally planned to cancel all existing contracts and demand a higher rental for the new two-reeler. However, hoping to prevent this move, the Theatre Owners' Chamber of Commerce protested, so a compromise was reached allowing a sufficient number of days in excess of the regular booking at the regular price, thereby making possible a greater gross than the territory would have shown with the increased prices.[40] However, individual theaters in the Minnesota and Eastern Pennsylvania regions took to the pages of the *Exhibitors Herald* to air continued grievances concerning their Chaplin contracts. Among the many specific cases was one that asked, 'Why is it that a holder of a contract only for *The Idle Class* is refused service because he did not use *The Kid*, when he never had a contract covering *The Kid*, and the local office had even refused in the first instance to sell him *The Kid*?' Another asked, 'Why is it that the local office refuses to serve anyone with *Idle Class* unless they first run *The Kid*?'[41] Other claims concerned only problems with contracts for *The Kid*, which were even more outrageous.

The Idle Class would be released in Britain in November, but before it even arrived, it had created considerable controversy. It seems that the rights to the film were purchased by the Film Booking Office (Arthur and Albert Chavering) for a record £50,000, forcing a high rental price then for theaters hoping to screen the film.[42] This not only caused protests but negative reviews of the film. In other words, it became clear that the reviews the film was receiving were based on a certain grumpiness around the high rental price and not the particular merits of the film itself. Arthur Weigall, writing in *The Daily Mail* exposed this tendency and wrote a frank appraisal of the film based solely on his own experience with it:

> It is not a picture which strikes a high artistic note as did *The Kid*; it belongs more to the class of Mr Chaplin's earlier work. It has no purpose other than to make one laugh and it is full of ingenious and novel little absurdities which keep one convulsed from start to finish.[43]

It's not clear when the transactions were completed, but Chaplin made two decisions about his own residence during 1921. The first was to rent a house for himself, instead of moving back to the Los Angeles Athletic Club after his divorce, and the second was to purchase a piece of property on which to build his own house in the future. The house he rented was at 6147 Temple Hill Drive in the Beechwood Canyon neighborhood and was named 'Moorcrest' by its architect, Marie Russak Hotchener. It was completed in 1921, so Chaplin would have probably been the house's first tenant.[44] He rented the place for $500 a month. Hotchener is important, not only for being a rare female architect, but because she designed several houses in the neighborhood, which came to be known as the Krotona Colony and, therefore, inhabited by followers of theosophy,[45] a religion which combined tenets of Buddhism and Hinduism, especially ideas such as spiritual evolution and reincarnation.[46] It's not clear whether Chaplin was a member of the Theosophical Society or just happened to rent the house that belonged to the group. As someone who was in a particularly soul-searching mood at this time in his life, however, meeting individuals like Max Eastman, infamous as a socialist who edited *The Masses* for many years, and taking some of their political ideology for his own, it wouldn't be surprising if he at least dabbled a bit. Even without this connection, however, the house was important for the people Chaplin hosted there and the experiences he had, for instance the all-night charade sessions with Eastman, Florence Deshon and others.

By 7 June, the date on which a classified ad for the sale of property next to Chaplin's on Cove Way (later Summit Drive) appears,[47] he had in fact purchased this property to build his own house. Building work on that house would not begin until 1922, however, and Chaplin would utilize his studio carpenters for the job, resulting in a grand house with structural problems that caused it to be deemed 'The Breakaway House' for most of its existence.

The next production for First National, Production No. 7, initially entitled *Come Seven*, is unique for several reasons. First, it is the only film that labels both Charlie and Sydney as co-directors of the film from the beginning (Charlie listed first, of course). Sydney was back working at the Chaplin Studios after a devastating couple of years trying to make it on his own. His twelve-picture deal with Famous Players-Lasky ended with one failed film. His airline went bankrupt after only nine months. His frequent business partner, Victor Levy, a totally unknown individual to Chaplin scholars, was the money behind most of his endeavors and probably the one who often led him astray, promising fast money for little investment and little effort on Syd's part, but, really, he didn't need Levy's assistance to get himself in real financial trouble. He was good at that all by himself and often got Charlie in trouble as well, especially in the area of taxes. By mid-1921, he was back on La Brea looking for something constructive to do and Charlie, ever the faithful brother, and still not having yet reached a point where he felt he could cast Syd aside, welcomed him back and even gave him some agency on this next project. Syd would take a significant role then in the last two First National pictures – but they would be his last acting roles working for his brother.

Another unique aspect of Production No. 7 was that it was in large part based on technology. This can be placed at the feet of Syd also. Unlike Buster Keaton, who demonstrated his facility with machines in nearly every one of his films, Chaplin habitually did not, although he did use an escalator in *The Floorwalker* (1916) and a revolving door in *The Cure* (1917). Some thought of Chaplin as a machine himself, due to his ratchety, syncopated gait, but never could his films be singled out for their demonstration of new or interesting early twentieth-century technology. Syd, however, was the tech go-to person in the family, the one who had kept a scrapbook on air machines when he was a boy and the one who had demonstrated for the first time the American Navy's submarine in his last Keystone film, *A Submarine Pirate* (1915). In Production No. 7 then, the machinery took the form of a workman's (hod carrier's) elevator, one constructed on the exterior of a building to facilitate transporting tools and equipment up and down the construction site. Gags involving this apparatus take up most of the first reel of the film. Another form of technology used in the film was nighttime filming, an innovation for Chaplin and relatively new for the film industry itself. This technology was used in the second reel, when Charlie is trying to board a tram and when he and his three saloon chums are singing harmony under the streetlamps, after leaving the drinking establishment. Also, it was the first Chaplin film to utilize artificial lighting in any form.

Perhaps another unique aspect of this film was that Chaplin began it on about 6 August 1921, prepared the story and looked for locations until 24 August and then halted filming to return to England for the first homecoming trip of his working life in America. The production reports state that 348ft of film were shot somewhere in there, but they do not indicate when or who might have been filmed or where they were filmed. One wonders if these reports were created to appease any First National boss who might have wanted to look at them, because nothing concrete happened on this project until 21 November, when Syd's name as co-director had been removed and rehearsal on the film began and would continue for five more days. First thing's first, however. Chaplin found himself tired and homesick by late summer 1921. *The Kid* had been released in his home country and he would be able to soak up an adulation peak caused by the success of his first feature. Making a semi-snap decision, he left Los Angeles by train on 27 August, with his brother Syd yelling after him something like 'Just don't let him get married.' He took along his valet, Tom Harrington and playwright and novelist Edward Knoblock, an American who had converted to British citizenship after the sinking of the *Lusitania*. Chaplin would spend most of his time away in his native England, but would also travel to Paris, where he was equally well-known and beloved and Berlin, where he was mostly unknown.

Chapter 7

The Kid Reception in Britain and Chaplin's Homecoming Tour (September–October 1921)

When Chaplin left for London on the SS *Olympic* on 3 September 1921, arriving on 9 September, controversy around his recent divorce was still occupying the American press. *The Des Moines* [IA] *Sunday Register* devoted two full pages of their Sunday magazine to Mildred Harris's court testimony during the proceedings that cast Chaplin as an insensitive husband.[1] Copyrighted by the International Features Service, the article would have appeared in newspapers throughout America's heartland, thereby presenting a figure of scandal, Chaplin-the-man, in contradiction to his beloved film persona, Charlie. Wes Gehring has also asserted, through the examination of contemporary news articles, that Chaplin himself was experiencing a sort of existential crisis, in that he had come to hate his Little Tramp persona such that he was having daydreams about leaving it behind.[2]

Possibly in answer to this concept of himself as a figure of scandal and to quell fears of the demise of his screen character, Chaplin released a 'promotional' travel book, *My Trip Abroad* (*MTA*) in February 1922 with Harper and Brothers Publishers, about four months after his return from the trip. The book then came to be serialized additionally in *Movie Weekly*, *Screenland*, and twenty-nine newspapers around the country (mostly second-string papers, such as the *Chicago News*, and the *New York Evening World*), as well as being translated into twelve other languages within ten years of its initial publication. Although the contract for *MTA* lists as its second point that the 'author is sole author and proprietor of said work,' the author being listed as Charles Chaplin, a Louis Monta Bell is listed as due to receive 1.5 per cent of Chaplin's 10 per cent of the profits in the fifth point of the contract 'for services rendered by him in connection with the writing of such work.' Correspondence between P.C. Eastment of McClure Newspaper Syndicate dated 19 October 1921 suggests the details of the financial deal regarding the serialization of *MTA* (which was to pre-date the publication by Harpers & Bros.). It should be noted that Chaplin's press agent at the time was involved:

> In accordance with our conversation with you and your representative Mr Carlyle Robinson, it is agreed that you will furnish material for a story of your trip abroad, to be written over your signature to us. [...] This story is to consist of approximately 50,000 to 60,000 words and is to be prepared by a thoroughly trained newspaper man and submitted to you and your representative for revision and approval before published in the newspapers.

A later letter from Eastment dated 16 February 1922 reveals some information on the way Bell may have gotten involved. Eastment writes 'I have no doubt that you are finding Mr Bell both very delightful and very useful to you and I feel pleased for your mutual sakes that our little business deal brought you together.' More important, though, is an unpublished typescript dated 24 May 1960 and titled 'Monta Bell' – a typescript found in among Chaplin's draft and manuscript material for *My Autobiography*. Chaplin's first line of this typescript serves as his admission in print of Bell's role. It reads: 'Monta Bell, the newspaper man who ghost wrote my book *My Trip Abroad*.' This evidence clearly shows that Chaplin did not write the book. Not surprisingly, there are no drafts of any kind for this work in the archives.[3]

An undated TLS in the Chaplin archive from Monta Bell to Chaplin written either in late 1921 or early 1922 indicates that Bell had accompanied Chaplin on the train from New York to Los Angeles after he arrived back from Britain on 10 October. He states in the letter that he had sent along three batches of copy for Chaplin to review, with about 30,000 more words left to write, which he believed would take about another week. Bell then asked Chaplin if he was serious about having a position for him at the Chaplin Studios. Of course, the answer to this question is evidenced by Bell's appearance as a cop at the beginning of *The Pilgrim*, Chaplin's final First National film. His tenure at the Chaplin Studios was short, but Bell went on to become a fine and respected director of such films as *Lights of Old Broadway* (1925) and *After Midnight* (1927). The book has been introduced first in this narrative to facilitate telling the story of Chaplin's journey, but also to show that the way he ended up telling the story with Bell's help served to promote a link between his Little Tramp character and himself that was designed to promote his film work – to get people out to the theaters to see his persona on the screen.

Often, travel narratives, usually organized chronologically, begin with a movement from personal crisis to nostalgia to embarkation. Chaplin's narrative follows this formula very closely. At the onset of the *MTA*, Chaplin's crisis is expressed in the three elements with which he chooses to open the work: 'A steak-and-kidney pie, influenza, and a cablegram.'[4] With the choice of these words, Chaplin has effectively related his increasingly alienated state to his readers, for each is a symbol of alienation inherent in modern life. The steak-and-kidney pie signals Chaplin's expatriate residence in America in that his desire for it heightens his growing feelings of homesickness for England. Influenza is a symbol not only of World War I, but the sickness engulfing the modern world following the war that took a great many lives as well, and Chaplin himself had just suffered from it. Finally, the cablegram is a symbol of modern technology, an innovation in communication that was designed to make the world smaller in some sense, but which could not help but emphasize the distance between persons, due to its physical reality of disjointed words and phrases on a small page. It was these three things, supposedly, which first set Chaplin on his journey.

Many of the stylistic choices in *MTA* seem to reflect the pervasive modernist theme of the work, namely alienation, isolation, and estrangement. While the fragmented sentences and one-sentence-long paragraphs of the narrative can easily be dismissed as evidence of the ghostwriter's (a journalist's) lack of literary prowess, a more useful rationale for their existence in the text is their apt promotion of the alienation characteristic of modern human life which the Little Tramp persona experienced in abundance. A typical example of this staccato text occurs on page seven:

Crowds. Reporters. Photographers. And Douglas Fairbanks. Good old Doug. He did his best, but Doug has never had a picture yet where he had to buck news photographers. They snapped me in every posture anatomically possible. Two of them battled with my carcass in argument over my facing east or west.

Neither won. But I lost. My body couldn't be split. But my clothes could and were.[5]

MTA had several printings in the States and was then translated and published in twelve countries on into the 1930s, with each edition bearing new photos of whatever Chaplin movie happened to be out at the time of its release. The contract for *MTA* guaranteed more than $15,000 for Chaplin and earned him much more than that.

Exhibition of a behavioral anomaly, specifically the revelation of exaggerated emotions, is a strategy the Little Tramp used in the films to solidify his persona. As expected, this strategy shows up frequently in *MTA*. The first instance of its utilization occurs at Max Eastman's house in New York, before Chaplin has even left the country. Eastman has invited a man called only 'George' to the affair, a prisoner on some sort of furlough from prison. Chaplin's brief interlude with the man that night is too emotionally overpowering for both it seems:

> We talk of George's future. Not of his past nor of his offense. Can't he escape? I try to make him think logically toward regaining his freedom. I want to pledge my help. He doesn't understand or pretends not to. He has not lost anything. Bars cannot imprison his spirit.
>
> I beg him to give himself and his life a better chance. He smiles.
>
> 'Don't bother about me, Charlie. You have your work. Go on making the world laugh. Yours is a great task and a splendid one. Don't bother about me.'
>
> We are silent. I am choked up. I feel a sort of pent-up helplessness. I want relief. It comes.
>
> The tears roll down my cheeks and George embraces me. There are tears in both our eyes.[6]

Such explicitly emotional scenes are so prevalent in this narrative that even the reviewers of the time took notice. A reviewer from the *Cleveland Press* writes on 10 March 1922, that 'few novels published recently contain as much real emotion and such thoughtful, sensitive observation as Charles Chaplin's account of his trip to Europe.'[7] And again, in Tracy Hammond Lewis's 'Charlie Chaplin Introspects' published in the *New York Telegraph* on 24 February 1922:

> There are few books which have been published lately that afford a more intimate acquaintanceship with their author than *My Trip Abroad* (Harper & Bros.), by Charlie Chaplin. Every thought and emotion experienced by him on his tour of Europe for a 'vacation' is set forth with the utmost faithfulness.

Chaplin's visit to the Garrick Club in London, which the ghost-writer relates in the text of *MTA*, a venue in which he meets up with what he terms 'the immortals,' J.M. Barrie, Gerald DuMaurier and other literati, demonstrates an instance that is made more Little-Tramp-like by vacillating throughout the evening between feelings of acceptance and utter rejection, moving back and forth between 'the indigent Cockney lad' and 'world-famous wealthy film star.' At one point, listening to the storytelling of one 'ruddy gentleman,' Chaplin reports that:

> Everyone is laughing at his chatter, but nothing seems to be penetrating my stupidity, though I am carrying with me a wide mechanical grin, which I broaden and narrow with the nuances of the table laughing. I feel utterly out of the picture, that I don't belong, that there must be something significant in the badinage that is bandied about the board.[8]

The ghost-writer for this text is successful in that the reader understands Chaplin's movement back and forth between roles, even to the point of 'trying on' words, such as 'nuances' and 'badinage' which would have been unfamiliar to a man with only two years of public-school education.

His experiences with H.G. Wells are plagued with the same sense of insecurity brought about by the need for constant metamorphosis. Even in an informal autograph-signing session, he is portrayed as analyzing the simple difference between his sweeping signature and Wells's 'small, hardly discernible style' as not just a difference in writing style but as a symbol of the large gap between them: 'I feel as though I had started to sing aloud before a group of grand-opera stars.'[9] Still, he finds himself posing for Wells, having dressed especially for the occasion:

> I try to explain my dress. Tell him that it is my other self, a reaction from the everyday Chaplin. I have always desired to look natty and I have spurts of primness. Everything about me

and my work is so sensational that I must get reaction. My dress
is part of it.[10]

Bell, as the ghostwriter of *MTA*, has done an excellent job of
exploiting Chaplin's tentativeness regarding social status, or at least
the audience's expectation of such a tentativeness. One such instance
occurs on board the SS *Olympic* when Chaplin goes to tea:

> The tea room suggests and invites social intercourse. Somehow
> there are barriers and conventionalities that one cannot break,
> for all the vaunted 'freedom of shipboard.' I feel it's a sort of
> awkward situation. How is it possible to meet people on the
> same footing? I hear of it, I read of it, but somehow I cannot
> meet people myself and stay myself.
>
> I immediately shift any blame from myself and decide that the
> first-class passengers are all snobs. I resolve to try the second-
> class or the third-class. Somehow I can't meet these people. I
> get irritable and decide deliberately to seek the other classes of
> passengers and the boat crew.[11]

This clear distinction Bell creates between his narrator Chaplin and
the upper-class passengers seems to reinforce a similar opposition
Chaplin often creates between the Little Tramp persona and his
particular antagonist in the films. The scenes with J.M. Barrie and
H.G. Wells recounted above are two other instances in *MTA* of Bell's
employment of this strategy and, as suggested above, each of those
leads to Chaplin's supposed attempt to metamorphose back and forth
between cockney lad and man of great wealth.

One of the 'names' Chaplin arranges to meet during his visit is
author Thomas Burke, a man who is largely unknown now, but at the
time of Chaplin's visit and on into the 1930s was immensely popular
for his lurid and suspenseful tales arising out of the transient dockside
neighborhood of Limehouse in London, populated by a mixture of

Chinese, Indian, and other immigrants, where Burke grew up. In the episode with Burke, he is to lead Chaplin on a tour of the Limehouse district, beginning at about midnight and walking well into the early-morning hours. Ostensibly, Burke is the guide of this particular tour, but, as Chaplin relates, the true guidebook for the tour is Burke's wildly popular collection of short stories, *Limehouse Nights* (1917). Chaplin explains his realization of Burke's particular *modus operandi*:

> He is silent and we merely walk.
>
> And then I awaken. I see his purpose. I can do my own story – he is merely lending me the tools. And what tools they are! I feel that I have served an ample apprenticeship in their use, through merely reading his stories. I am fortified.
>
> It is so easy now. He has given me the stories before. Now he is telling them over in pictures. The very shadows take on life and romance. The skulking, strutting, mincing, hurrying forms that pass us and fade out into the night are now becoming characters. The curtain has risen on 'Limehouse Nights,' dramatized with the original cast.[12]

Although one of the main reasons he had indicated before traveling to Europe was his heart's desire to attend the premiere of *The Kid* in London, in fact, he did not get to attend such an affair. That day had already passed. So, instead, Chaplin busied himself with meeting 'the immortals,' as he termed them, visiting old haunts (some in the middle of the night) and entertaining his vast audiences. The day before he left for Paris, 17 September, Chaplin entertained fifty lucky Hoxton children at the Ritz Hotel, performing impromptu impersonations for them and accepting their gift of a box of cigars and a flower bouquet.[13] This would mark the first of many occasions in which the comedian would attempt to return to his roots through the poorer children of London and alleviate their suffering with entertainments for an hour or so.

Arriving in Paris on 18 September by train, Chaplin was chased from the station to the Hotel Claridge on the Champs Élysée by hordes of female fans. Once there and safe, he called for solitude, suggesting to his admirers that he could make no exceptions for any of them. Obviously, even at this date he was considering a French setting for an upcoming film, 'I want to take up a new role and therefore must study,' he said. 'I am very glad to be visiting France again after many years.'[14]

Before he returned to London, Chaplin then traveled to Berlin (with Carlyle Robinson as his companion), where he was little known, and recognized not at all. Being three years after the war, Chaplin would have wanted to take the opportunity to introduce his films to Germany, whose citizens would become some of his staunchest fans (and harshest critics) in the years to come. On this occasion, he met German film star Pola Negri, among a group of German dignitaries, for a photo-op that almost seemed prophetic, for Negri and Chaplin would become engaged just a couple of years later, if only fleetingly.

Chaplin returned to Paris on an Instone[15] Airline machine in the morning and was able to attend the premiere of *The Kid* there at the Trocadero on 21 September, organized by the American Committee for the Devastated Regions. Douglas Fairbanks and Mary Pickford were on hand for the event, which attracted 6,000 enthusiastic attendees (the theater's capacity).[16] He had been placed together with Parisian beauty Cécile Sorel for the evening, who escorted him throughout the proceedings following the film. The evening's host, M. Léon Daudet capped the evening with the exclamation, 'Long live the king, Charles!' This proclamation was followed by several others from stars in attendance, including Musidora, who offered, 'For God, Carlos Chaplin!'[17]

Leaving Britain on 8 October, Chaplin was reported as having almost missed his connections, 'at half-past ten he was still in bed, but within 35 minutes he had breakfasted, made his toilet, said "Good-bye" to the host of friends at the Ritz and dashed into a taxi.'

He arrived at Waterloo station five minutes before his scheduled departure time, but the train was ten minutes late, giving him time to pose for the crowds from his carriage window, receiving a few kisses from a brave girl or two and offering up his characteristic smile. He soon departed from Southampton on the SS *Berengeria*.[18]

Back in the States for a month, Chaplin received a letter from Monta Bell, written in November 1921, suggesting that at least this cog in Chaplin's publicity machine was aware of the need for immediacy and for getting the travel narrative as a whole released to the public before too much time went by:

> I will wire you immediately upon receipt of any information as I believe it imperative that the book be published at once if there is to be any real sales. An ordinary book by you would go well at any time, but this one concerning a recent trip is more or less in the nature of news and it soon gets stale.[19]

Perhaps due to this sense of urgency, Bell uses the fragmented sentence liberally, especially to create an atmosphere for moments of excitement and anxiety.[20]

Chaplin arrived back in Hollywood then on Halloween (31 October). He met sculptor Clare Sheridan, a niece of Winston Churchill, at a dinner party that night and entertained her and her son Dickie at the studio on 2 November. An agreement was made at that point for Sheridan to sculpt a bust of Chaplin. Sheridan's husband had been killed in France, and so, as a single mother of two (only one child was with her in California), she was immediately considered a possible match for Chaplin when their friendship was discovered by the press. Sheridan accomplished the bust in just three days, then Chaplin suggested that the three of them (Chaplin, Clare, and Dickie Sheridan) take a camping trip at the beach, which they did for a week beginning 6 November. They were chased home by carloads of fans on 11 November and the Sheridans took off for New York soon after.

When asked about the possibility of her marrying Chaplin, Sheridan remarked: 'Man proposes; woman disposes,'[21] thereby leaving each to interpret those words however he or she saw fit. Chaplin did not meet Clare Sheridan again but kept the bust she had sculpted of him in his domicile until his death.

Meanwhile, Chaplin and company were back in the studio as of 21 November to complete *Pay Day*, and spent the first five days rehearsing and waiting for sets to be prepared. Filming started in earnest on 26 November, with the scene outside the Bachelor's Club at night – one of the several night scenes shot for the film. The next two days, retakes of the club's exterior and rain in the street were taken. The players for this scene included Syd, Henry Bergman, Loyal Underwood, Al Garcia, and John Rand. One report noted that this amounted to the revival of an 'ancient custom,' that of poor men's clubs' backyard quartets, of which Chaplin, given his expressions, was obviously singing the tenor part.[22] On 29 November, the coffee stall and rainy street were shot, and the next day was spent cutting and finding locations. The story and locations were prepared on 1 December. The next day the streetcar scene at night was shot on Glendale Boulevard with a 'mob' of extras.

Back at the studio on the third, Chaplin filmed rainy street scenes again, and between 4 and 9 December, sets were prepared, with some shooting on the 10th in a bedroom set with Chaplin and Edna Purviance (a scene that didn't make the final film). The next week was devoted to preparing the story and more sets. On 19 and 20 December, Chaplin shot the scene in the Little Tramp's dining room with many lively cats. By the next day, filming was being done in the dining room, bedroom, and bathroom sets – chronologically, some of the final scenes of the film. The domestic scenes in the Little Tramp's residence now featured old Keystone stalwart Phyllis Allen as his wife (she appears on the reports as of 21 December). The scene in the hall set is filmed on 22 December. Cutting was done on 23 and 24 December and then, with only one day off for

Christmas, they were back constructing sets on the 26 through 28 December. Filming of Phyllis Allen in the Hall set was completed on 29 December, including close-ups. The last two days of 1921 and the first week of 1922 included no filming due to Chaplin being ill, yet he was able to attend a New Year's Eve dinner at the home of Mr and Mrs Thompson Buchanan, with a guest list that included Mr and Mrs Rob Wagner, and Elinor Glyn of *It* fame. After rehearsing on the 9 January, filming resumed the following day at the pay shack set on the studio grounds. For the first reel of the film now being shot, Mack Swain would join the cast.

Filming in the street was achieved on the 11 January and then shots were taken of the building exterior (the construction set) on 12 January. Film was shot out on the street at Cahuenga and Metro the next day and on De Longpre and La Brea the day after that – this last most likely being the scene, now again quite famous, in which Chaplin is walking along with his wife, is passed by a young lady and turns completely around to take note of her. After another day rehearsing, filming began on the building construction set on 16 January for several days until 24 January, when filming was halted to work out the scene's ending. Two more days were then spent filming on the construction set. Cutting began 27 January, but the next day, Chaplin was being filmed on the construction set alone. This was followed by three days of cutting. On 2 February, they were back on the building exterior set and then doing retakes of some of the night scenes the next day. Two more days were spent filming on the building exterior set, with filming completed on 7 February.[23,24] The film, titled *Pay Day* in its final form, was turned over to First National on 23 February 1922.[25] Chaplin celebrated this, presumably, with a visit to the studios of ballerina Anna Pavlova, in town on her tour of the western United States at the time. *Pay Day* was released in theaters on 2 April 1922. Chaplin had kept the basic storyline secret until mid-March at least, keeping visitors to the studios at a minimum during the filming,[26] He attended the preview screening at the Florence Theatre in Pasadena in late March, garnering a fifty-two-second ovation from the surprised audience.[27]

One Los Angeles critic, labeling the film 'a document for the laboring man,' insisted this was because Chaplin wrote his own stories, with the result that so doing resulted in 'a greater scope of expression with an expansion of personal ideas.' In other words, the self that Chaplin expresses in his photoplays 'is a hypersensitive soul that reacts positively and quickly to the sorry or happy condition of other people's affairs.'[28] While Tally's Kinema did good business with the film in week one, the second week slacked off quite a bit, unlike the two Chaplin films before it. The Strand Theatre in New York, however, was still doing good business the second week of *Pay Day's* run, with Harriette Underhill noting in her column on 3 April that a person should go early to the film, in order to beat the rush: 'It took two traffic cops to direct the motor cars up to and away from the Strand yesterday and two more to keep the sidewalk cleared for passersby.'[29] The critic from the *New York Herald* provided a typical review of the film: 'this picture of what a bricklayer does with the pay he holds back from his wife looks like an assemblage of funny odds and ends tacked together to furnish a pay day for the comedian's company.' However, by the body of the review, he seems to have changed course a bit, noting that 'the scenes in which Chaplin joins in a barroom quartet, get mixed up with the overcoat of another anti-Volstead vocalist and tries to get on several crowded trolley cars are among the funniest ever shown on the screen.'[30] Critics overall were mostly split on the film's merits, with most agreeing at least that it was simply not long enough.

One of Chaplin's assignations came to a tragic end on 2 February 1922. Early that Thursday in Greenwich Village, building manager Nevins Lamb noticed a smell of gas in his apartment building as he was sweeping the stairwell, but failed to do anything about it. By evening, the smell had become so strong that others were alerted, and the source was found to be the apartment of Florence Deshon, amour of several years of both Chaplin and Max Eastman. Deshon was discovered in bed with her nightclothes pulled over her street clothes, the gas valve opened slightly, but a window also partly opened, a factor that resulted in confusion over the actress's actual intensions. Deshon was still breathing at the time she was found and immediately transported to St. Vincent's Hospital. Still alive on Saturday 4 February, Eastman donated his blood to her for a transfusion, but it was too little too late, for she died that evening.

Rumors ran rampant to the effect that Deshon and Eastman had engaged in a noisy row over his imminent departure for Europe to attend the Genoa conference there and that this was perhaps the reason for her drastic action. Her death was not ruled a suicide, but simply death by asphyxiation (although in one report she had overdosed on Veronal as well) and Eastman released a statement concerning his certitude that the death was completely an accident and had nothing to do with him. Chaplin's name was linked to the actress in these reports, although there was no indication from them of the seriousness of their affair, one that supposedly ended with the miscarriage of a malformed baby (believed by some to have been simply an aborted baby).[31] This experience had weakened Deshon's health and overall demeanor; she had recently left Hollywood following the demise of her career there and was hoping to work on the legitimate stage once in New York. Her funeral was held at Campbell's Funeral Home (later made famous by its location as Valentino's funeral in 1926) on 6 February and was buried on Long Island.[32] Although the press was certain that some animosity over 'possession' of Deshon between Chaplin and Eastman would have driven an irreparable wedge between the two men, in fact they remained friends down through the years.

Perhaps it was Max Eastman who began the trend of analyzing Chaplin and his Little Tramp persona as a figure of the avant-garde and, therefore, as a great artist. Eastman, through his close acquaintance with Chaplin, came to include both in memoirs about, and an analysis of, the actor in his books, *A Sense of Humour* (1921) and later, *Heroes I Have Known* (1942) and *Love and Revolution: My Journey through an Epoch* (1964). In *A Sense of Humour*, Eastman compares Chaplin's art to Aristophanes and analyzes it accordingly. A month later, the writer of 'Screen,' in the *New York Times* got on board with his column, 'A Clown a Poet,' devoted to French philosopher Elie Fauré's analysis of Chaplin. Fauré, in a two-part article for *The Freeman*, suggested that Chaplin was a poet, 'even a great poet, a creator of myths, symbols and ideas, the discoverer of a new and unknown world. [Therefore, he] thinks cinematographically' and 'organizes the universe into a cineplastic poem and flings forward into the future, in the manner of a god.'[33] And so, the fashion among the literati became thinking about the Little Tramp metaphorically, symbolically and mythologically. Reading these pieces, Chaplin could only have come to take himself too seriously perhaps.

By March, perhaps because his next film release was a long way off, the press decided to start a discussion on Chaplin's romantic life once again and many feature articles appeared with photos of the various linkups he was alleged to have had. May Collins, with whom Chaplin had not been involved for almost a year, was included, perhaps because she had just signed a contract with Metropolitan that forbade her to marry for three years, thus leaving him out in the cold (or so they surmised). Edna Purviance, with whom Chaplin had not been linked romantically since at least 1917, was included, as was Claire Windsor, a young starlet who was rumored to have had herself kidnapped to get Chaplin's attention (he offered a reward of $7,000 for her release). Another woman considered was Lila Lee, whom Chaplin was most recently reported to have been dancing all night with at the Ambassador Hotel's Cocoanut Grove.[34] Edwin Schallert, in fact, centered his article in this vein around one night at the Cocoanut Grove in which all these women were in attendance, with some even wearing the gifts that Chaplin had given them – the silver fox for May Collins and the ermine stole for Claire Windsor.

All of these women were accused of boosting their careers through their time spent in Chaplin's company, whether innocently or not.[35] Had she still been alive, Florence Deshon might have been added to the list, even though only Grace Kingsley of the *Los Angeles Times* had ever mentioned her in such a capacity.

On 8 March, Chaplin took Little Tramp imitator Charles Amador (AKA Charles Aplin) and Western Features Production to court to try to halt their efforts to release Little Tramp-esque films. Western had two films with Aplin completed and ten more on the way. Chaplin's complaint was that the films and Aplin himself try to imitate 'his world famous costume and mannerisms.' The costume was described in court documents as 'a decrepit derby, ill-fitting vest, ill-fitting coat, trousers and shoes much too large for the wearer. Also a flexible cane, which this actor is wont to swing while acting.'[36] Aplin countered by claiming that the character was a common vaudeville type and if anyone had a claim to it, that would be Billie Ritchie, another Karno player making films in the United States. He claimed that Chaplin was only jealous and had no claim on the character or his costuming.[37] The hearing was set for 6 April and to be held in Superior Court Judge Crail's courtroom, but it was postponed by both parties until 21 April and then continued by Judge Crail until 28 April, due to a delay in receiving Chaplin's paperwork from the East. Chaplin received a temporary injunction to prohibit the release of the first two Aplin films but was back in court 5 October 1923 trying to make the injunction permanent. In fact, he was still trying as of 19 February 1925, when yet another hearing took place to try to stop this imitator and his films. By this date, both parties had waived a jury trial and were looking for a decision by Judge John L. Hudner himself. The case was finally decided in Chaplin's favor on 11 July 1925; the release of any Charles Aplin film was prohibited, as well as Charles Amador being banned from ever again using the stage name of 'Charles Aplin.'[38]

1 April, just one day before *Pay Day* was to be released, Chaplin began work on his final film covered by the First National contract, initially title *The Tail End*, for obvious reasons, but that soon became *The Pilgrim*, a film that would take Chaplin out of this period of his career with a huge bang.

Chapter 8

Finishing Up the Contract: *The Pilgrim* (1923) and Its Controversies

Perhaps an inference or two can be made by the fact that Chaplin went back to the studio on April Fool's Day to get started on his final film required by the First National contract. The final product ending up being four reels in length, creating further problems for Chaplin – so much so that drastic measures had to be taken at a time when Chaplin and company should have been enjoying their last days filmmaking under the gun, so to speak. Rather than going quietly, however, Chaplin chose to leave this contract in a blaze of glory.

Titled *The Tail End* on the production reports, Production No. 8 was also referred to as *At Large*[1] and *The Western* before it officially became *The Pilgrim*. As Robinson has noted in his Chaplin biography, typed notes about the story exist for this, and only this, First National production. He surmised that this may be due to the presence of Monta Bell (a journalist) at the studio, who may have volunteered to type them up and/or it may indicate that Chaplin, with his sights set on United Artists productions, decided to change up his mode of devising scenarios. Whereas throughout his career thus far he had the habit of rehearsing on film and taking a day to several days off to 'talk story,' Robinson duly notes that in both the *Pay Day* and *The Pilgrim* productions, the production reports give evidence of very little downtime for such things – meaning that Chaplin must be working from notes for a scenario made before production began.[2] One interesting scene that did not make it into the final version involves Charlie being vamped by a dance hall girl in the scene in which he goes there to take back the stolen money (in this case 'the bank' of a poker game):

> The toughs … try every sort of trick to get the money away from Charlie but he outwits them at every turn … They put their heads together and decide that the way to get the money is to use a woman on him, so they enlist the services of Nell the Dance Hall Queen. She is to vamp Charlie and get the money. There is a comic love scene, Charlie falling for the vamp, she in turn falling for him, becoming converted and telling him she'll come to church and dance for him.[3]

The original cast list included Mack Swain as the Bully instead of the Deacon, Phyllis Allen as the Deacon's wife and Carl Miller as Edna's brother.

The first day of production was spent looking for locations, preparing the story and sets and the next week the same. On 10 April, filming began with the interior of the railroad depot, a scene in which Monta Bell has a role. The scene was filmed on a prepared set at the studio. The next day filming moved out to the Saugus railway station to film the exteriors of the same scene, continuing there through 13 April. Others in these scenes were Syd Chaplin, Miss Evans and Frank Liscomb, as well as Chaplin himself. On the 14 April they were back in the studio, rehearsing and waiting on costumes. Then, using natural light, filming was done again at the Southern Pacific yards, this time filming the Little Tramp's arrival into town as the new parson. The plot had been set in motion by a newspaper article that the Little Tramp happened to read as he was figuring out how to escape the police's notice, being a fugitive. The prop article, which still exists in the archive, reads 'The Reverend Mr Brown, new parson for our church, will arrive in town Sunday morning. He will be met at the Station by Sheriff Smith and a committee from the church.'[4]

Mack Swain, Edna Purviance, Loyal Underwood, Syd and others made up this committee. On 17 April the company moved to the Raymond Depot in Pasadena for filming and to the street near Eagle Rock. On 18 April Chaplin began shooting the interior of the church and the Little Tramp's uneasy first sermon there. Of course, the church needed to be filled with people and so a long list of forty-one extras inhabited the production report for that day, including Miss Marion Davies, although it is impossible to find her in any of the existing footage of the scene. She was also present during shooting on 19 April. Raymond Lee, the young boy who Chaplin had used in *The Kid*, during the boxing match with Jackie, was brought on board 21 April and appears in the scene as the misbehaved boy who scratches his head a lot. Filming this scene continued until 22 April, which was spent cutting 'factions,'[5] (Chaplin Studios' slang for scenes or sections of film) and then was picked up again on 24 and 25 April filming on the same set, but in the ante room, where the Little Tramp toys with stealing from the collection boxes.

During the shoot, there were developments at United Artists. On 21 April it was announced that United Artists president, Dennis O'Brien, had concluded negotiations to form 'Allied Corporation,' a vehicle for releasing films only, and which would not enter the production field in any way. It would handle the release of independent productions only, with Max Linder Productions being one of the first such independents to be offered distribution through this new concern. The company was to have the same board of trustees and the same stockholders as United Artists.[6]

Between 26 and 29 April no shooting was done, due to waiting for sets. The week of 1–6 May was spent waiting for parts for the studio generator, preparing sets and rehearsing a new character part. The next week was spent 'getting the faction ready,' or more understandably, preparing the story, sets and rehearsing. On 15 May, Stage 3 at Universal studios was utilized, where the interior of a Pullman car was shot, but the next three days were spent again in preparing the faction. On 19 May they were back at Universal, this time shooting the exterior of the prison and again the interior of the Pullman. A note in pencil on this day's report stated Rothacker (the company that made Chaplin's prints after he turned them over to First National) 'developed print sample.' The 20 to 22 May were spent waiting for the set and 23 May rehearsing, with filming being taken up again between 24 and 27 May at the studio on the interior of Edna's living room set. New cast members for this set of scenes included Kitty Bradbury (from *The Immigrant*), Chuck and his son 'Dinky' Dean Riesner, and Tom Murray, who played the sheriff. The scene between Charlie, Syd and 'Dinky' is film gold, but legend has it that the Chaplin brothers had to go to great lengths to get 'Dinky' interested in playing a slapping game with them.[7] Little Dean Riesner also received a bit of publicity for his role, in the same way that Jackie Coogan had received it, except that 'Dinky's' role was smaller. Young Riesner had been born during the filming of *A Dog's Life*, making him 4 years old at the time of *The Pilgrim's* filming, just as his predecessor Coogan had been. With his success, Chaplin was becoming known for spotting youngsters likely to make a go of it in the film business.[8]

On 29 and 30 May, the scene moved to the kitchen of Edna's house, where Chaplin's Little Tramp becomes involved in decorating a cake as only he could. Between 31 May and 5 June, filming moved to Edna's living room set at the studio, then 6 through 8 June, Chaplin was cutting the scene. On 9 June, the company moved to Culver City and shot at the swimming pool. Chaplin was cutting on 10 June and the company rehearsed on 12 June. Shooting was done back on the living room set the next day and the day after that was given over to rehearsing. And again, they were back in the living room set for two days, followed by another day of cutting on 17 June. Two days later they were shooting on Ventura Road for part of the day and then in the church ante room and telegraph office sets back at the studio.

Chaplin called in sick on 20 June, then spent three days hunting for locations after that. On 24 June the company shot on location in

Pasadena and at Eagle Rock. The next day shooting was done at the studio on the interior hall set. They were back on location again on 27 and 28 June, this time at Sawtelle, where the exterior of Edna's house was filmed. The next day filming took place back at the studio on the exterior of the church, the church ante room and the kitchen sets (this last of Edna's house). After one more day in the kitchen, the report for 1 July notes 'Roscoe San Fernando,' the meaning of which is not clear, but could simply mean some property owned by Roscoe Arbuckle in the San Fernando Valley, since there is no location with this name.

This location continued to be filmed up to and following the 4 July holiday. In fact, this is the final scene of the film in which Charlie is arrested at the border by Tom Murray, the sheriff, and then let go. Finding that Mexico, however, seems to be filled with bandits, the Little Tramp leaves the film with one leg in America and one in Mexico, as if that is the safest option. Then on 6 July the location moved to the church in Newell, which becomes the exterior of the church in the film. The next day, they filmed on location at Universal City and at Western Street, and between 8 and 14 July new sets were prepared. When the café set was completed, filming began and ended there on 15 July, which is noted as officially the last day of filming.[9] Post-production work, such as creating the titles, is greatly elucidated by a list of these contained in the archives, which numbers thirty-eight pages. Only the first page is in Syd Chaplin's handwriting, but one can see from his lengthy title suggestions a sort of metamorphosis of the titles as they come out, at the end consisting of mostly three or four words and sometimes less. The brief title card, a hallmark of Chaplin silent films, is shown then to be a purposeful element of them.

This happened to be just in time because Lord and Lady Mountbatten arrived in Hollywood on their honeymoon on 18 July. More fondly known as Dickie and Edwina, during their extended three-month honeymoon the couple visited the royal courts throughout Europe and began to make their way across the American continent, stopping for a Yankees baseball game, a day at Coney Island and every proper honeymooners' location Niagara Falls, before moving further west. The couple were supposed to stay at Pickfair with Fairbanks and Pickford, but by the time they arrived, the Fairbankses were in New York for a film premiere. The Mountbattens were persuaded to stay at Pickfair anyway and wanted for nothing. Charlie was assigned to be their host during this time, which, of course, led to the famous, and infamous, little film *Nice and Friendly*, put together by Chaplin during the couple's visit. He also screened *The Pilgrim* for them one night, even though it had yet to be released to the public.[10]

Nice and Friendly, according to David Robinson, utilized anyone available. Besides the young couple (who played the distressed damsel and her lover), the cast included Robert Thompson, a local businessman, as the villain; Jackie Coogan as Mountbatten's valet, Thorogood; Chaplin himself as both villain and Little Tramp-esque savior; and two other couples, Mr and Mrs Neilson and Mr and Mrs Pell, each in small parts.

After the Mountbattens left Pickfair, Charlie sent them a telegram in which he related that 'it was a gorgeous time while you were here and someday we may repeat it,' and that he was 'working arduously to complete [the film],'[11] and would send it to them. Lord Mountbatten was still emoting about the film in a letter to Charlie in 1965: 'As I told you the other night, of the many hundreds of wonderful wedding presents we received, this one on our honeymoon was the most dramatic and historic and the one of which Edwina and I have always been the most proud.'[12]

However, *The Pilgrim* was not released until 26 February 1923 due to some disagreements between Chaplin and First National about what he expected to be paid for the film. Chaplin sent a long cable to Nathan Burkan, his lawyer, on 25 September that stated he had received a letter from Harry Schwalbe demanding he submit Production No. 8 on contract. Schwalbe stated that John McCormick and Sol Lesser had viewed No. 8, when Chaplin stipulated in his cable that they had viewed *The Pilgrim*, which he was calling 'a special' rather than the actual eighth production. Chaplin claimed that Schwalbe had already offered him a 50/50 percentage on the profits after $250,000, with $200,000 on submission of the film. Chaplin instructed Burkan that if First National now reneged on this deal, to remind them of the many ways they had already broken the existing contract, for instance, regarding film copyright about which Burkan had already given them a thirty-day notice. Of course, Chaplin wished to have the legal opportunity to release the four-reeler with United Artists.[13]

In fact, the disagreement was so dire this time that Chaplin cut together a two-reeler, known today as *The Professor*, which included various and sundry cut footage from *Sunnyside* and *Shoulder Arms* plus a dosshouse scene shot during the *Sunnyside* production in 1919 that included one of Chaplin's favorite gags involving trained fleas. Recently, Arnold Lozano of the Roy Export office in Paris, the Chaplin family organization, has pieced together the story, which others had only surmised over the years. In fact, the cutting continuity and storyline of *The Professor* exists in the archive, suggesting not only that *The Professor* had been cut together as an actual two-reeler, but that, through an examination of other documents, it played an important part in Chaplin's negotiations with First National involving more money for his four-reeler, *The Pilgrim*. As Lozano notes, the idea of using *The Professor* as a bargaining chip meant that Chaplin fully intended to submit the two-reeler as his final film for the contract, and then either sell the four-reel *The Pilgrim* as a special, or simply as an additional film with First National, which would mean more money.

The synopsis of *The Professor* as it exists in a document in the archives, suggests that the first scene is the one in which the Little Tramp is walking down the street with three boys and then encounters his unseen wife at home, a cut scene from *Shoulder Arms*. This is followed by a lengthy scene of Chaplin attempting to shave a man (played by Albert Austin) – a cut scene from *Sunnyside* – extended out to the point at which Edna arrives at the grocery counter and is getting a bit irritated waiting for Chaplin to serve her. Since a portion of this scene does actually appear in *Sunnyside*, and Chaplin needed only unused footage, one wonders if that portion of the scene could have actually been the version with Zasu Pitts in her one and only try-out. In the next scene, Chaplin receives a letter from the army extolling its virtues such that he decides to join up, so naturally, this is followed by the scene in the Examining Office, again with Austin and Purviance, in a cut scene again from *Shoulder Arms*. Because he fails to pass the physical, Chaplin takes to the streets and develops his talents in other directions, so now the scene in the dosshouse is featured, in which the Little Tramp has become Professor Bosco, the tamer of a flea circus, but not a successful one. The final scene is Bosco back on the street snapping his whip at a dog that has taken his fleas, both characters dissolving into the night.[14]

Chaplin took a brief holiday in San Francisco, arriving on 6 November at the Palace Hotel.[15] He was the guest of automobile man Don Lee, who wined and dined him and took him out on his yacht.[16] He fended off rumors that he was engaged to actress Eleanor Boardman, who Chaplin claimed he had met only a few times.[17] Mostly, he was hoping to rest and ready himself for the next adventure – making films for United Artists.

Syd had been sent east with Arthur 'Sonny' Kelly,[18] now working for the studio, to band together with lawyer Nathan Burkan and on 13 November sent a cable to Charlie which reported that Harry Schwalbe was anxious to settle the negotiations amicably and suggested that both films, *The Professor* and *The Pilgrim* be submitted together to First National, that way, the two-reeler could close the contract and a price for the four-reeler could then be negotiated without the strictures of the original contract. He noted, however, that the Executive Committee of First National would want to view both films before any agreement could be made and Chaplin disagreed with this requirement, insisting on a release document signed by both himself and a First National representative for each film before they could be viewed. Syd told his brother that if he wanted to shelve *The Professor*, then he (Syd) would want permission to allow First National to view *The Pilgrim* without a signed release. He advised that Chaplin's initial offer was untenable: 'Schwalbe stated that there is absolutely no profit for the First National in releasing for 30 per cent and therefore I suggest you increase the distribution allowance to them in the case of *The Pilgrim*.'[19] On 14 November, Charlie cabled back that he did not want to submit both pictures to First National, however he would consider allowing them to view *The Pilgrim* without the signed release, but not the two-reeler. He wrote that he would consider a modified distribution percentage of 65/35, but that all other aspects of the deal must adhere to the modified contract for *The Kid*. If First National did not want *The Pilgrim* after viewing it, then Syd was to submit *The Professor* as the final film, but without their viewing it first.[20] Meanwhile, Chaplin previewed *The Pilgrim* in Los Angeles the week of 13 November and was buoyed by the response.

On 20 November, Syd wrote his brother that First National was now offering 50 per cent of the gross derived from the United States and Canada over $280,000, with an immediate payment of $100,000 upon delivery of the print[21] (Syd had a positive with him, but the negatives were back in Hollywood). On 21 November Chaplin cabled that the offer was 'ridiculous' and that Syd should deliver *The Professor* sight unseen and contact Hiram Abrams of United Artists about distributing *The Pilgrim*.[22] On 30 November, ads began appearing for the film coupled with photos of Chaplin in costume as the parson taken by famed photographer James Abbé. Critics such as James W. Dean, whose preview of the film was carried throughout the country, noted that he was given very little of the film to write about, the clip ending with Charlie meeting the reception committee in the town where he is to fill the opening for a parson. Dean explained that this sketchy outline of the story precluded him from making any more global observations.[23]

On the 6 December negotiations were still not going well, as evidenced by a cable from Chaplin to Syd in New York (addressed 'Snyder Chaplain'), which stated that the First National executive in Los Angeles 'failed to offer suitable conditions for promotion of special four-reel feature *Pilgrim*,' so Syd was to go ahead and submit *The Professor* as the eighth and final First National film to complete the contract.[24] The same day, the studio manager Alf Reeves cabled Syd with more information. He outlined to Syd and Burkan what was happening at the studio:

Information President and Secretary both saw Chief [Chaplin] personally. We asked four hundred thousand payable two hundred thousand now, seventy-five thousand six months and one hundred twenty-five thousand received previously. Percentage sixty-five thirty-five including foreign rights. They countered with offer sixty-five thirty-five percentage, one hundred thousand on delivery, fifty thousand six months, United States and Canada, no foreign share. This is not acceptable. Matter stands.[25]

Chaplin himself cabled Syd the next day, writing that since no agreement had been reached, *The Professor* should be delivered as the final film of the First National contract.[26]

By 15 December, however, things were looking up again and Chaplin cabled his brother that the deal outlined in his cable of 13 December (not in the archive) was acceptable as long as the '$75,000 in six months' part of the deal could be obtained.[27] A cable on 20 December from Reeves to Syd reported that Schwalbe wanted delivery of *The Pilgrim* by 26 December. He asked Syd to have them deposit $155,000 into Chaplin's Italian account by that date and two negatives would then be delivered upon the bank's notification that the funds had been deposited. Syd could then also deliver the positive he possessed.[28] On the 21 December the conversation in Reeves's cable to Syd turned to taxes and referred to Norton, possibly Chaplin's tax lawyer, and the fact that he had taken in a lot of money that year (1922) and would have big taxes to pay.[29] By the next day, however, more controversy had arisen because Chaplin had noted that there was no communication about the $75,000 being guaranteed, nor was their language about Chaplin's demand to retain oversight of exhibitor's contracts, so he was again threatening to dump everything and submit the two-reeler.[30]

Finally, a new contract, which included *Pay Day*, was signed 8 January 1923, with the negatives being turned over 9 January. *The Professor* was relegated to the annals of history and as revealed earlier, was only cut back together recently after a thorough study of the documents. The new contract guaranteed $250,000 (of which $125,000 had already been paid) plus 50 per cent of all funds over $500,000, with $75,000 paid in advance coming from this 50 per cent. For *Pay Day*, they agreed to pay 50 per cent of all funds made over $250,000, retroactive to this date and which, as of 31 December 1922, was $30,000. Other sections of the contract in existence for *The Kid* were to apply to this agreement as well.[31] Finally, the film was released to the public 26 February 1923. Unlike the other films in the First National collection, however, this one would prove to be controversial. The deal was announced at last in the 20 January 1923 issue of *Motion Picture News*, which reported that a screening of the film for First National executives some six weeks before at Bim's Standard Theatre in New York, plus a preview for the public at Gotham's Theatre in the same city, left no doubt as to the film's bankability.[32]

Reception of the film was, like the other films since *The Kid* and *The Idle Class*, mixed. San Francisco was doing enough good business for its Lyceum Theatre to run the film for three weeks, but other cities experienced a drop-off after a mere three days. The Kinema in Los Angeles reported an enthusiastic crowd initially. One critic noted

'*The Pilgrim* is funny. It has a maturity and subtlety about it that comes with age. There even are several moments when the audience fails to catch the humorous situation. It is funnier than it casually seems.'[33] The memorable highlights of the film were the most often touted in its reviews: the David and Goliath pantomime that Charlie performs in the church; the derby hat being used to ice a cake at the parishioners' house; and the metaphoric ending, in which Charlie is released by Sheriff Smith into the borderland of Mexico but, finding it a dangerous place, straddles the border between Mexico and America as he moves into the horizon. Perhaps at least one more scene should have been added to the list – the remodeled dance hall scene in which Charlie adapts his parson's hat into a ready-made cowboy hat, his tunic into a Western costume, then holds up the gamblers in the joint, to recoup the money Chuck Riesner's character had taken from Edna and her mother.

Then there was the American Midwest, that chose to use the film's release as an opportunity to protest against what they considered a disrespectful depiction of the clergy, and efforts were made to ban the film, or at least relieve it of its objectionable parts. On 3 April, the Ministers' Association of Atlanta declared the film 'an insult to the gospel,' as well as 'an attempt to ridicule the Christian religion,' and demanded the film's withdrawal in Atlanta, a demand that fell on deaf ears.[34] Clergy from Venice, California, made a similar demand.[35] The clergy in Walla Walla, Washington, also had similar feelings but, unlike Atlanta, they were considered and G.E. Terhune, owner of the Arcade Theatre there, decided to cancel the film completely.[36] In Mason City, Iowa, a group of twenty Ku Klux Klan members protested outside the Palace Theatre against the screening of the picture. In this city, however, the clergy had already looked it over and had no objections, even attempting to mollify the Klan members, but to no avail.[37] In Spartanburg, South Carolina, the Klan (specifically the Daniel Morgan Klan) brought up similar objections to the film to the local Better Films Commission, causing the screening of the film to be stopped by Mayor Floyd. The reporter writing about the situation offered the stance of his publication:

> We should think the Christian religion, which has come down through the ages, unmasked and unshrouded in mystery might be spared the spirit of intimidation and threat in these latter days. If the Protestant ministry cannot stand without an escort of the Klan, it has lost the Spirit of the Master.[38]

Then Will Hays, the recently appointed film censor, intervened and passed the film, with only a few minor changes. The theater owners of Philadelphia persuaded Hays to intervene due to the outcry from clergy and subsequent censorship from state authorities that was also taking place there,[39] a censorship that was later denied by Pennsylvania Board of Censorship chairman Harry L. Knapp, who claimed they only 'softened' the film a bit.[40] The state of Ohio went ahead and cut the film itself, 'First reel: Cut out scene where flask is exposed in deacon's hip pocket and scene where Chaplin takes the flask. Second reel: Cut out two close-up burlesque scenes of choir singing. Fourth reel: Cut to five feet scene of Chaplin held over candle flame.' The reporter of this action expressed his indignation that the citizens of Ohio couldn't even see a choir burlesqued: 'Who are choir singers that they should not be burlesqued any more than a butcher, a baker, or a candlestick maker?'[41]

Back in November 1922, Polish actress Pola Negri published her memoir in installments in the newspapers, including a chapter on her meeting of Chaplin in Berlin the year before. She claimed to be dining with two American friends Mr and Mrs Kaufman at the Palais Heinroth, a fancy restaurant on the Kurfürstendamm, when her host jumped up and signaled to two American men standing in the doorway of the restaurant, one of them being Chaplin, to join them at their table. Negri claims she had heard his name many times before this, had seen his photo in a movie magazine, but had never seen his films. She didn't understand what all the fuss was about. Chaplin was then seated by Miss Negri, and his companion, Carlyle Robinson, also joined the table. According to Negri's account, Chaplin not only admitted knowing Negri and her work, but claimed she was the most beautiful woman in the world and the person he most wanted to meet on this trip. Negri and Chaplin were thrown together at every occasion over the four days of his Berlin side trip and, according to her, enjoyed the freedom inherent in not being recognized as a film star. Just three short months after his trip, Chaplin's films began to be shown in Germany for the first time, and at the writing of Negri's memoir, he had become the most popular comedian in Germany in the interceding year.[42]

By 25 November, the media was reporting that Chaplin and Negri were engaged. They had reconnected at the Actor's Fund Pageant in at the Hollywood Bowl, Saturday 7 October. At the announcement of their imminent nuptials, Negri denied the engagement, while Chaplin would neither confirm nor deny, saying that Miss Negri needed to be the party deferred to in regards to this question.[43] In the succeeding months, the couple posed for photos here and there, the most famous of which took place on the grounds of the Pebble Beach Golf Course near Monterey, California, on 28 January 1923, where Chaplin presented the actress with a sparkly ring. However, by 1 March, Negri had ended the engagement due to a misunderstanding created by the press, a quote from Chaplin that said she was too poor to marry. Chaplin visited Negri that evening and persuaded the actress that he had made no such comment, so the engagement was back on within twenty-four hours.[44] The reconciliation was short-lived however, for the engagement was broken off for good in the last week of June, although not announced until on 28 July, when Negri had replaced him with tennis player Bill Tilden.[45] The unraveling of the Chaplin-Negri relationship was not announced, but the two attended the reopening of the Cocoanut Grove at the Ambassador Hotel on 26 July in the company of others, Negri with Tilden and Chaplin with actress Leonore Ulrich. Negri explained that she found Chaplin too temperamental and too mercurial: 'In my opinion, Mr Chaplin should never marry. He has not any quality for matrimony.'[46]

Chaplin had been thinking about life after his First National contract for a long time, but mid-February 1922 marks a point at which some of his intentions hit the media. It was reported that he had decided to promote his loyal leading lady to this point, Edna Purviance, as a star.[47] Initially, this announcement was accompanied by the formation of Regent Films, a separate company Charlie and Syd created to exploit Purviance, and there were hints that Syd would direct her in a starring role under the Regent Film banner. Her films would be produced at the Chaplin Studios. But these plans went by the wayside, when Syd began to get character parts in several films at other studios and left the employ of his brother once again. Chaplin decided to stick with his idea of promoting Edna Purviance, however, only she would appear in a film he directed, and it would be his first for United Artists. He started talking to the press seriously about this in November 1922: 'My contract has expired and I'm going to direct a picture. A real drama about a woman. I have a lot of drama corked up in my system and one must have an outlet.'[48]

Lots of ink has been spilt about who or what inspired various characters within United Artists Production No. 1, which was initially titled *Public Opinion*, then *Time and Destiny* and finally *A Woman of Paris*. Chaplin had been thinking about this Purviance-centered film for some time and it has been argued that many of his affairs during this time could be considered 'laboratory love affairs,' or dating as scientific study.[49] Chaplin scholar Wes Gehring has made this argument in his book *Charlie Chaplin and A Woman of Paris* (McFarland, 2021), suggesting that even Chaplin's alleged engagement to Pola Negri was one such relationship. David Robinson, as well as Gehring, underscores the assumption that the model for Purviance's character Marie was a combination of all these women, but mostly based on early twenties cultural icon Peggy Hopkins

Joyce, a renowned woman of the time who created the template for the likes of Kim Kardashian today. Chaplin had both made her acquaintance and supposedly dated her in the few short weeks she spent in Hollywood before Mary Pickford made her feel unwelcome and she removed to Paris.

Gehring discusses the acclaim attached to Adolphe Menjou in the role of Pierre Revel, the womanizer that audiences around the world came to love and adore, but he mentions nothing about who might have been the model for this character. Robinson, however, points to Henri Letellier, a French publisher and bon vivant whom Joyce had had a relationship with during her man-eating years, a personage that Chaplin himself had met briefly during his homecoming visit to Europe in Fall 1921.[50] In fact, early story notes use the names Peggy and Letellier for Purviance's and Menjou's characters.[51] While Letellier might have been a bit of a model for Revel, it is also likely that French comedian Max Linder was a great influence on Chaplin's idea of the ideal French playboy. Chaplin and Linder had become firm friends, despite the language barrier, during Linder's two forays into the Hollywood film business, first in 1917 and then again in 1919 through 1922. In the latter period, the two men had lived right around the block from each other and were often photographed together at film premieres and other events, when they found each other's company more fulfilling than the latest female interest. Linder was a notorious bachelor, one who kept his romantic affairs out of the press in France (and in America), until he was felled by 23-year-old Ninette Peters, whose mother was a courtesan and the daughter of another courtesan. Clearly, Linder's general treatment of and experience with women greatly matched that of Pierre Revel. This idea is reinforced by the fact that Chaplin welcomed several French assistants onto his set, to help him with authenticity, including Linder colleagues Jean de Limur and Robert Florey. Assistant director on the film, Eddie Sutherland, was responsible for hiring Menjou, whose authenticity in the role was heightened by his French ancestry.[52]

The production began on 27 November 1922 (the studio records report the onset as 15 August 1922) and officially ended 29 September 1923. As Chaplin had begun to employ first in *Pay Day*, and to a greater extent in *The Pilgrim*, this first United Artist production began with story notes and a more fleshed-out scenario than Chaplin had used to write his earlier shorts (Monta Bell continued on the set in the role of 'literary editor'). There are notes, both written out and typed, of every scene in the film. Some offer alternate endings – a wedding between Marie St. Clair and Pierre Revel in one and a meetup between Marie and Pierre, when Pierre is driving through the countryside and Marie and Jean's mother have taken the orphan children in the cart on a picnic. In this one, Pierre tells Marie that he is now free to marry and will remain so, waiting for her to change her mind. The actual ending, in which Pierre in his chauffeur-driven car and Marie hanging off the back of the cart, pass on the road without either noticing or acknowledging the other provided a less predictable ending that worked harder in garnering the many 'like real life' reviews it received at the time. The production came in at a cost of $351,853.03 for its eight reels.[53]

Having wrapped *A Woman of Paris*, Chaplin decided to take a trip to Detroit, Michigan, and visit, among others, Henry Ford and his Cadillac factory. George W. Stark reported that Chaplin had not graced the city with his presence for eleven years, when he had appeared there with Karno's London Comedians in the skit 'The Wow-Wows.' His visit was a big deal. His party, made up of Hiram Abrams and Fred Schaefer of United Artists and Arthur 'Sonny' Kelly, acting as Chaplin's personal representative, was met by a committee of 'first citizens,' motorcycle officers to handle the traffic, and railroad police in the station to clear a way for the Chaplin party to exit the train. He was driven to the Statler Hotel in an open car, and was recognized all along the route. At breakfast in the hotel, he met the press, commenting to them that he had wanted to direct a serious picture like *A Woman of Paris*, because he needed a break from comedies: 'I thought the break in the awful monotony of being funny would help me freshen my mind and I think it has. But I will never give up making comedies. With me it is a serious business, this business of being a funny man.'[54] A large photo on the front page of the *Detroit Free Press* on 16 October shows Chaplin standing between Henry Ford and his son Edsel. He also visited three high schools and three primary schools before he was given a tour of the Highland Park Ford plant by the two Fords. During his encounters with the children, Chaplin mentioned that his next film would be a comedy, 'I will be in snow up to my neck, up in the Klondike with bears and everything.'[55] And, so, Chaplin has made one of his first mentions of what the film that sanctified his tenure with United Artists, *The Gold Rush* (1925) would encompass.

Epilogue:

On into the Future:
Chaplin's Remaining Life and Work

C haplin's many risky experiments in *Woman of Paris* would not be attempted again, at least not in the same way. He would return to the Little Tramp persona now for four (and some say five) more features, starting with *The Gold Rush*, his own personal favorite, in 1925. Meanwhile, First National (now Associated First National Pictures, Inc.), assuaged their Chaplin losses by reincorporating again on about 6 May 1924, calling themselves this time First National Pictures, Inc. and taking on, finally, the film production business. With the advent of sound film in 1927 and the success of *The Jazz Singer* for Warner Bros. however, First National's time and dominance had passed, and Warner Bros. was able to purchase a majority of First National stock and take it over by 27 September 1928. Warner kept the First National name on a particular strand of its films then until 12 July 1936, when the company and name were finally dissolved.

Before initiating *The Gold Rush* production, Chaplin secretly married Lita Grey, the former Lillita McMurry of the heaven scene in *The Kid*, in Guaymas, Mexico on 26 November 1924. Lita, like Mildred, was not a mental match for Chaplin and was intimidated by characters such as Albert Einstein, whom she might have to play hostess to on occasion. The two were grossly mismatched from the start. However, they had two sons together, Charlie Chaplin, Jr., born 5 May 1925, and Sydney Earl Chaplin, born 30 March 1926. Charlie, Jr. lived painfully under the shadow of his famous father and took to alcohol as a relatively young man, dying in 1968 at the age of 42. He left one daughter, Susan Maree. Sydney followed his father into showbusiness, having inherited an incredible voice from some music hall singer deep in his Chaplin ancestry, winning a Tony on Broadway for his role in *Bells Are Ringing* opposite Judy Holliday. He also starred on Broadway with Barbra Streisand in *Funny Girl* as Nick Arnstein. He married ballerina Noelle Adam in March 1960 and had one son, Stephan, but the marriage didn't last. He can be seen playing opposite his father in *Limelight* (1952) and *A Countess from Hong Kong* (1957). In the late 1980s, he was the owner of a restaurant called 'Chaplin's' in Palm Springs, a celebrity hangout. He married Margaret Beebe in 1998.

Lita Grey and Chaplin were divorced 25 August 1928 in the messiest public divorce in history to that time. Pamphlets of the court testimony were published and sold on the streets, detailing the sordid nature of Grey's charges against Chaplin. As with Mildred, Chaplin took off for New York again to wait things out, leaving behind an unfinished film, *The Circus*, that had just suffered a major fire in the circus tent set at the studio. Chaplin went grey and lost so much weight during this period that all were concerned with both his mental and physical health. However, he returned to Hollywood in late August, finished *The Circus* and went on to begin filming *City Lights*, a silent film with a synchronized soundtrack,[1] which was shot and released well after sound films took over the film business.[2] With this film, Chaplin added 'composer' to his list of credits, for he wrote the score for this and every subsequent film in his oeuvre. His new leading lady was the recalcitrant Virginia Cherrill, destined to become Cary Grant's first wife (for a very short time). When the production wrapped, Chaplin took off on a sixteen-month tour of Europe and Asia to promote the film because he was insecure about its acceptance due to its still being silent. He needn't have worried.

On his tour, Chaplin visited England, Germany, France, China, Japan, Bali, Java, Sri Lanka, and Singapore, bringing back with him an even deeper and more mature sociopolitical consciousness that would invade his films to come. Brother Syd had left the film business in 1929 after a personal scandal that resulted in his being blacklisted and unable to get a job in any aspect of the industry, so he took up residence in the south of France, in Nice, where he met up with brother Charlie during this tour. The brothers were more estranged from each other than at any other time in their lives so far, and the tension could be felt by both men during this tour.

Back in Hollywood in June 1932, Chaplin embarked on his first actual writing assignment, a five-installment travelogue[3] of his trip commissioned by *Woman's Home Companion* that was due as soon as he could get it finished. It was truly the first such effort he made wholly on his own, as evidenced by the drafts of the series in the Chaplin archive. Chaplin received $50,000 for the project. Hard on the heels of this endeavor was Chaplin's next film production, *Modern Times*, featuring another new partner for the Little Tramp, fondly referred to as 'the gamine,' played by Chaplin's new girlfriend Paulette Goddard. The film demonstrated Chaplin's new eye for political messages in his films, for the Little Tramp played the everyman worker during the Great Depression, who seemed to be at the mercy of Fate no matter how hard he worked or under what incredible circumstances. Others in the cast included Hank Mann and Chester Conklin, both from the Keystone days; Tiny Sandford, who would be cast again in *The Great Dictator*; and Gloria de Haven, daughter of Carter de Haven, who was on her way to becoming a big Hollywood star. This would be Chaplin's last silent film, and its construction to some felt like an anthology of many of Chaplin's old gags from films as far back as the Essanays. Until his next film, this would be his greatest money-maker.

Chaplin and Goddard took another trip to Southeast Asia between 17 February and 3 June 1936, after *Modern Times* was completed and supposedly were married somewhere there, although no documentation of the marriage exists. Still, they lived together as man and wife until things began to sour in about 1938, marked transparently by Chaplin's long stay in northern California with writer John Steinbeck and other creative types. He was looking desperately for a suitable story for Goddard, trying a regency romance, a story of Napoleon at Elba (for which he enlisted Alistair Cooke to help write), and several stories about young lovers in Bali, all of which never amounted to anything. He settled finally on a satire of Germany's controversial leader at the time, Adolf Hitler, not really knowing or understanding when he embarked on the project the incredible horror the man was subjecting Jews and marginalized groups to in his country and throughout Europe. This would be Chaplin's first talking picture and the first for which he had to deal with the industry unions, an adaptation that was especially difficult for him because he was used to doing his own hair and make-up and sometimes that of the other actors in the piece, but with the unions, this was no longer allowed. Production started 1 January 1939 and soon Syd, who was at loose ends after the death of his wife Minnie from breast cancer in 1936, came back to the US at his brother's request to help with the project. Writer and social activist Dan James became one of the several assistant directors on the film. Half-brother Wheeler Dryden, who, after several rejections by his two brothers, had finally been welcomed into the family fold by this time, was another one.

Goings-on at the Chaplin studio were closely guarded, which was usual for a Chaplin picture, but this time they also had to deal with threats against Chaplin and the studios from parties sympathetic to the Nazi cause in America. President at the time, Franklin D. Roosevelt, sent his man Harry Hopkins to make sure the production came off without a hitch, because Roosevelt wanted it made. Although Goddard had a major role in the film, the couple were estranged, creating a lot of tension on the set. Chaplin also hired character actors Henry Daniell, Reginald Gardiner, Billy Gilbert, and Jack Oakie to fill out his cast. Hank Mann and Chester Conklin were again cast in small parts. *The Great Dictator* premiered in New York on 15 October

1940 and in Los Angeles in November. It became Chaplin's biggest moneymaker, earning him $5 million worldwide.

A trying few years were on the horizon for Chaplin at this point in his life and career. He was between projects and so, distractions of one kind and another began to cause him problems – problems so dire that the reverberations can be felt to this day in some cases. In 1941, he got the idea to re-release some of his best silent features with a soundtrack, essentially with Chaplin narrating what was going on in each scene. He began with *The Gold Rush* and re-released it in May 1942.

Paulette Goddard received a divorce from Chaplin on 4 June 1942, but Chaplin hadn't waited for this document to start placing himself in trouble with women again. This time it would be a young actress named Joan Barry, whom he placed under contract in June 1941, thinking that her red hair and freckled face would be perfect for an Irish story he was considering making into a film, *Shadow and Substance*. Unfortunately, Chaplin chose unwisely, for Miss Barry was not only a bit unstable, but had been spending time with men such as J. Paul Getty while she was with Chaplin. This became important due to a paternity suit involving Chaplin, regarding a child that Barry believed was his. Also, because he had brought Barry to New York with him at one point (against her wishes, as Barry testified), he was brought up on charges under the Mann Act, which basically said that a woman could not be brought across state lines for the purposes of sex. Chaplin's FBI file was growing by leaps and bounds at this time also, due to various political speeches involving Russia and her need for support on the Eastern front of World War II. All in all, these events added up to bad news for Chaplin. His trial(s) brought on by Barry occurred 10 February 1944 to 4 April 1944 (Mann Act case) and then 13 December 1944 to 2 January 1945, when a hung jury demanded a retrial. The retrial began on 4 April 1945 and ended in Barry's favor on 17 April 1945, largely because the results of a paternity test that Chaplin willingly took were disallowed as evidence. The test proved Chaplin was not the father of Barry's child, but because it was disallowed, he was ordered to pay for a child not his.

Two other items important to this time were his meeting and marrying his fourth and final wife, Oona O'Neill (they married on 16 June 1943 in Carpinteria, California) and his steady work on a new screenplay, that of *Monsieur Verdoux*. Oona O'Neill was the 18-year-old daughter of famous American playwright Eugene O'Neill, author of such works as *Long Day's Journey into Night*, *Emperor Jones* and *The Iceman Cometh*, among many others. He would never meet Chaplin or any of his eight grandchildren. The story behind the film that would become *Monsieur Verdoux* was one of a French murderer named Henri Landru, who married older women and eventually killed them and burned them in an outdoor incinerator, to take their money. The film's production lasted from 21 May to 5 September 1946, with comedy stars such as Martha Raye (who stole the show) and William Frawley in the cast. Again, Chaplin needed French assistants to guarantee the authenticity of the film, and this time employed Robert Florey as one of them. Not only was the film panned by critics and boycotted by audiences, but Chaplin was subjected to a long and trying press conference supposedly on the film, but really on his political endeavors that were causing him more and more trouble. This was the era of McCarthyism and the House on Un-American Activities trials (HUAC). Chaplin was never brought in front of the committee but subjected himself to many long interrogations by the authorities outside of court that were just as serious.

Chaplin and his young wife Oona began having children in 1944, their first being Geraldine, who is still an acclaimed actress in her own right. Geraldine was followed by Michael, then Josephine and finally, for the United States, Victoria. Having these wonderful children and a beautiful loving wife in his life now worked wonders on lessening the effect of bad reviews on Chaplin and the critical and biased media. Logically, it was time for a family film and so *Limelight* came into being. It was a story of a down-and-out English music hall comedian named Calvero and the young ballerina whose life he saves at the start of the film (she had tried to commit suicide) and who eventually reaches stardom and the arms of a younger man over the course of the story. Calvero dies in the last scenes of the film. It was a family film in that Chaplin's two older sons by Lita Grey, Charlie, and Sydney, had parts; his half-brother, Wheeler Dryden, had a part; and even his four youngest children can be seen in the early moments of the film as a drunk Calvero attempts to open the door of his apartment building, without much luck. Chaplin's last Hollywood film, *Limelight*, filmed from 19 November 1951 to 25 January 1952, with young British actress Claire Bloom in the lead female role.

By the time *Limelight* was released, Chaplin's reputation overall was pretty much beyond hope of repair with the American public and so, even though it was truly a family film, many theaters across the country simply boycotted it. Perhaps for this reason, Chaplin desired strongly to travel to Britain for the premiere of the film there, hoping for greater appreciation by the citizens of his native land. On 17 September 1952 the Chaplin family – Charlie, Oona and four young children – left New York Harbor for London. His re-entry permit was rescinded on 19 September and the Chaplins decided not to protest the issue. They found themselves arriving in London without a home to call their own.

Finally, on 5 January 1953, Charlie Chaplin and his family moved into the Manoir de Ban in Vevey, Switzerland, on the shores of Lake Leman. It would be Chaplin's final home. But from this venue he would entertain the great and the near-great for another twenty-two years. He would lose brother Syd in 1965 and had lost his oldest son seven years before that. This year he would also publish *My Autobiography*, a project he had been working on diligently for many years. He would make two more films, *A King in New York* in 1957, a film made in response to the ill-treatment he received in America during the last ten to twelve years there, and *A Countess from Hong Kong*, released in 1967, which was the adaptation of a story about a

White Russian countess fallen on hard times that he had initially worked up for Paulette Goddard back in the 30s. The film starred Sophia Loren and Marlon Brando, but perhaps the greatest moments in the film are provided by Patrick Cargill as Hudson, Brando's valet, and Margaret Rutherford as Mrs Gaulswallow, an elderly passenger on the ship. This was also Chaplin's only film in color, and the second film in which he had no real acting role. After a tennis accident this same year, Chaplin slowed down and spent much of his time receiving well-deserved accolades of one kind and another from all over the world. He and Oona had four more children in Switzerland, Eugene, Jane, Annie and Christopher, who was born when his father was 73 years old.

Hollywood called him back in 1972 to receive a lifetime achievement Oscar, which he took some time deciding whether he would do. Supposedly, he was convinced to make the trip, because it would allow him to investigate a new type of film camera that he was hoping to use on a new project, a quasi-religious film entitled *The Freak*, which would feature his young daughter Victoria in the role of an angel living in the real world. Chaplin made the trip to great acclaim from both East- and West-coast audiences and the ovation at the Academy Awards that he received is still the longest on record for a lifetime achievement awardee (it is also the only time that presentation was made as the final one of the broadcast). Five years later, on Christmas morning 1977 around about 4.00 am, Chaplin drew his last breath. His private funeral was held in Vevey at an Anglican church and he was then buried in the tiny cemetery, Cimitière de Corsier-sur-Vevey on 27 December on a very cold and rainy afternoon. Not long after, two men, Roman Wardas and Gantcho Ganev, a Pole and a Bulgarian respectively, decided to disinter Chaplin's body 1 March 1978 and held it for ransom, until it was recovered by authorities on 17 March. Wardas received four years in prison, Ganev only eighteen months.

Oona Chaplin joined her husband on 27 September 1991. Her eight children with Chaplin all survive as of this writing and have contributed grandchildren and great-grandchildren aplenty to the Chaplin fold.

All of Chaplin's films are in existence except the Keystone film *Her Friend the Bandit* and all have been restored at least once, if not more. Roy Export, S.A.S., the Chaplin family organization based in Paris, continues to guard his legacy and bring his work into the future for new generations to discover and enjoy. He would be happy to know that in the year 2022 his films have been well cared for, are screened around the world with the music he wrote for them, and that his work and legacy have been appropriated by many new young artists in media he never could have imagined or understood.

Notes

**Chapter 1: Negotiating with First National, Leaving Mutual Film Corp.,
Building the Chaplin Studios**

1. 'The First National Circuit Had,' *Motography* XVII (19) 12 May 1917, p.1022.
2. 'National Exhibitor's Circuit Organized,' *Motography* XVII (19), 12 May 1917, p.974.
3. 'Chaplin to Get $1,075,00.00,' *Motography* XVIII (2), 14 July 1917, n. p., Pressbook, CHACHAA.
4. 'Rothapfel Heads Exhibitors Combine,' *Motion Picture World* 12 May 1917, p.935.
5. William Parker, 'Capitalizing Personality,' *Motion Picture News*, 19 September 1914, p.51.
6. William Parker, 'Capitalizing Personality,' *Motion Picture News*, 19 September 1914, p.52.
7. 'Chaplin Formally Signs Contract with Circuit,' *Motion Picture News*, 21 July 1917, p.384.
8. TLS Sydney Chaplin to Charlie Chaplin, 3 July 1917, New York, CHACHAA.
9. 'Chaplin Formally Signs Contract with Circuit,' *Motion Picture News*, 21 July 1917, p.384.
10. 'Chaplin to Strive for Quality,' *Moving Picture World*, 21 July 1917, p.431.
11. 'Chaplin Formally Signs Contract with Circuit,' *Motion Picture News*, 21 July 1917, p.384.
12. Grace Kingsley, 'He Earns a Rest,' *Los Angeles Times*, 2 October 1917, p.III: 3.
13. Qtd. in David Robinson, *Chaplin: His Life & Art*. New York, McGraw-Hill, 1985, p.162.
14. 'Chaplin May Enlist,' *Los Angeles Evening Post-Record*. 7 June 1917, p.2.
15. 'Peer and Movie Star Have Row,' *Honolulu Advertiser*. 21 August 1917, p.5.
16. 'British Embassy Clears Chaplin,' *The Morning Telegraph (Washington, D. C.)*. 8 August 1917, n. p., Pressbook, CHACHAA.
17. 'Charlie Chaplin in Real Life is Islands Visitor,' *Honolulu Star-Bulletin*, 10 October 1917, p.11.

18. 'Yesterday Morning,' *Honolulu Star-Bulletin*, 13 October 1917, p.14.

19. 'Charlie Chaplin Says Hilo and Volcano Are Great,' *Hilo Daily Tribune*. 16 October 1917, p.5.

20. 'Buy Liberty Bond, Chaplin Urges,' *Honolulu Advertiser*, 17 October 1917, p.II:12.

21. 'Buy Liberty Bond, Chaplin Urges,' *Honolulu Advertiser*, 17 October 1917, p.II:12.

22. Letter John Jasper, Lone Star Studios, Los Angeles, 3 July 1917, to Syd Chaplin, Claridge Hotel, New York City, CHACHAA.

23. 'Charlie Chaplin Will Build Own Film Plant,' *Los Angeles Times*, 16 October 1917, p.II:1.

24. 'Chaplin's New Studios,' *Moving Picture World*, 10 November 1917, n. p.

25. 'Will Go Ahead,' *Los Angeles Times*, 21 October 1917, p.V:1.

26. Qtd. in 'Attempt of Hollywood Citizens to Force Removal of Studios Fails – City Council Votes Chaplin Permission to Build Plant,' *Trade Review*, 3 November 1917, n. p., Pressbook, CHACHAA.

27. G.P. Harleman, 'Chaplin Breaks Ground for New Studio,' *The Moving Picture World*, 24 November 1917, p.1178.

28. 'Work to Be Started at Once on Buildings of Chaplin Studio,' *Los Angeles Times*, 2 December 1917, p.1.

29. 'Chaplin's Hollywood Motion Picture Plant, Most Complete in West, Nears Completion,' *Exhibitor's Herald*, 20 December 1917, n. p., Pressbook. CHACHAA.

30. 'Three Cameras Catch Chaplin's Start,' *Motion Picture News*, 9 February 1918, n. p., Pressbook. CHACHAA.

31. 'Another Important Addition,' *Los Angeles Evening Express*, 16 January 1918, p.15.

32. Grace Kingsley, 'Charlie Chaplin Begins Work in a New Studio,' *Los Angeles Times*, 20 January 1918, p.III:1.

33. Elsie Codd, 'The New Chaplin Studio,' *Pictures and Picturegoer*. 20 January 20 – 2 February 1918, p.102.

34. Daily Production Report, Charlie Chaplin Studios, January 15, 1918, CHACHAA.

35. 'Charlie Chaplin Gives New Year's Party at Hotel Alexandria,' *Exhibitors Herald*, 19 January 1918, p.12.

Chapter 2: First film *A Dog's Life* (1918) and the Third Liberty Loan Tour

1. Conclusive identification provided by Steve Massa.

2. Granville Redmond (1871–1935) was a California impressionist, who fell upon hard times during World War I and decided to supplement his income with acting in silent films for which he had some facility given his disability. Chaplin not only utilized him in several films but gave him an

unused room in the studio rent free in which he could paint whenever he was not on set. Chaplin would sit silently and watch him when he had the chance: 'Redmond paints solitude, and yet by some strange paradox, the solitude is never loneliness.' (Qtd. in Will Dudding, 'Overlooked No More: Granville Redmond, Painter, Actor, Friend.' *New York Times*, 8 April 2021. https://www.nytimes.com/2021/04/08/obituaries/granville-redmond-overlooked.html).

3. Syd Chaplin found himself between film contracts at this point in his career, having left his Keystone contract at the end of 1915 and occupied himself with supporting Charlie's career first at Mutual and now at First National. He did not appear in Mutual Films but seems to have altered his plan a bit with First National, appearing in four of the eight films of the contract. In 1919, just as Charlie was beginning to have trouble, Syd also got a bit itchy and went looking for adventure, becoming involved in the first domestic airline in the United States, the Syd Chaplin Aircraft Corporation, a dressmaking firm with his wife Minnie, Sassy Jane, and his own film contract with Famous Players Lasky, which he failed to complete. For more about Syd Chaplin and his up and down life, see my book, *Syd Chaplin: A Biography* (2010).

4. CAL, 'The Very Latest about Charlie Chaplin.' *Red Letter*, 6 July 1918, n.p., Pressbook. CHACHAA.

5. CAL, 'The Very Latest about Charlie Chaplin.' *Red Letter*, 6 July 1918, n.p., Pressbook, CHACHAA. Also, 'Would Steal Charlie's Stuff.' *Los Angeles Times*, 3 February 1918, III:19 A.

6. Letter J.D. Williams, First National Exhibitor's Circuit, Inc., NY, 26 February 1918 to Syd Chaplin, Hollywood, CA. CHACHAA.

7. 'C. Chaplin Dug Up Riotous Dance Hall Bowery for His New Picture,' *Dallas Times Herald*, 31 March 1918, n.p., Pressbook. CHACHAA.

8. 'Charlie Chaplin and W.J. Bryan.' *The Evening Index* [Greenwood, SC], 9 March 1918, p.1. Although he would duck out of the tour early due to exhaustion, his initial planned dates and locations were: two meetings in Virginia 11 April, two in North Carolina 12 and 15 April, one meeting in South Carolina 15 April, Nashville, Tennessee on 18 April, Bowling Green, Kentucky on 19 April, Memphis, Tennessee on 20 April, Greenville, Mississippi on 22 April, New Orleans on 23 April, Port Arthur and Beaumont, Texas on 24 April, Galveston and Houston on 25 April, Austin and San Antonio on 26 April, Waco and Dallas on 27 April, then Augusta, Georgia on 16 May and Macon and Atlanta, Georgia on 17 May. Quite a grueling schedule. ('Capital Is Not Included in Chaplin's Itinerary,' *Evening Star* [Washington, D.C.], 29 March 1918, p.4)

9. 'Another Chaplin Delay.' *Variety*, 5 April 1918, n. p., Pressbook. CHACHAA.

10. Daily Production Reports, Charlie Chaplin Film Co., 15 January 1918 to 9 April 1918, CHACHAA.

11. It was announced on 3 November 1917 that Rothacker Film Manufacturing Company had achieved the contract to reproduce Chaplin prints, considered one of the if not *the* most lucrative of such contacts ('Rothacker to Print Chaplin Releases.' *Motography*, 1 November 1917, p.946).

12. 'Prints Being Made of "A Dog's Life" at Rothacker Plant.' *Exhibitor's Herald*, 20 April 1918, p.23. The film's copyright number is L12302, and its record contains only a short story description. LOC-MPCDC.

13. 'Chaplin and Pup Portray Two Tramps in "A Dog's Life."' *Moving Picture World*, 6 April 1918, p.116.

14. 'World Crew Sees "A Dog's Life,"' *Moving Picture World*, April 27, 1918, p.546.

15. 'Chaplin's New Comedy Breaks Many Records,' *Moving Picture World*, 4 May 1918, p.725.

16. 'Chaplin Film Extends Its Run,' *Motion Picture News*, 1 June 1918, p.3278.

17. 'Chaplin's Famous Little Dog is Dead,' *Motography*, 25 May 1918, p.1000.

18. 'A Present for Chaplin, *Moving Picture World*, 31 August 1918, n.p., Pressbook, CHACHAA.

19. *A Dog's Life* Memorial Album, CHACHAA.

20. Richard Sutch, 'Liberty Bonds – April 1917 to September 1918.' https://federalreservehistory.org/essays/liberty-bonds. See also, Lawrence D. Schuffman, 'The Liberty Loan Bond, *Financial History*, Spring 2007, p.18–19.

21. 'Final Drive for Liberty Loan Marked by Big Results,' *Motion Picture News*, 30 June 1917, p.4059.

22. '[The most important item],' *Deseret News* [Salt Lake City, UT], 6 April 1918, p.25.

23. Stephen Moloney, 'Mary Pickford, Chaplin and Fairbanks Given Great Reception,' *Salt Lake* [City] *Herald Republican*, 3 April 1918, p.10.

24. 'Crowds Greet Movie Stars at Union Station, *The Omaha Daily Bee*, 5 April 1918, p.11.

25. 'A Mighty Trio in Aid of Third Liberty Loan Drive,' *Moving Picture World*, 13 April 1918, p.250.

26. Mae Tinée, 'Mary and Charlie and Doug Mobbed by Admiring Host,' *Chicago Tribune*, 5 April 1918, p.1.

27. 'Immense Throng Greets Stars of Filmdom Here, *Harrisburg* [PA] *Telegraph*, 5 April 1918, p.1, 22.

28. Lea Stans, 'The Great Chaplin-Pickford-Fairbanks Liberty Loan Tour of '18.' https://silentology.wordpress.com/2018/08/29/the-great-chaplin-pickford-fairbanks-liberty-loan-tour-of-18/

29. Katherine Pratt, 'An "Illuminating Post": Silent Stars Support the Third and Fourth Liberty Loan Campaigns,' 26 September 2018, *The Unwritten*

Record Blog [*National Archives*]. https://unwritten-record.blogs.archives. gov/2018/09/26/an-illuminating-post-silent-stars-support-the-third-and-fourth-liberty-loan-campaigns/

30. 'Fairbanks and Chaplin Thrill Wall Street Hosts,' *New York Herald*, 9 April 1918, p.16.
31. '20,000 Throng Wall Street to Hear Movie Stars Tell How to Win War,' *New York Tribune*, 9 April 1918, p.8.
32. 'Golden Harvest of Loan Subscriptions Garnered by Fairbanks, Pickford and Chaplin in Philadelphia,' Pressbooks, CHACHAA.
33. 'Philadelphians "Dig Deep" as Filmdom's Stars Urge Success for Liberty Loan.' *Evening Public Ledger* [Philadelphia, PA], 9 April 1918, p.1.
34. Letter Charles Lapworth, San Francisco to Charles Chaplin, Los Angeles, 14 February 1919. CHACHAA.
35. C. L. Keep Report on Rob Wagner from the UCLA Library Special Collections available at https://hollywoodoblivion.wordpress.com/rob-wagners-script-archive/. UCLA-SC-RWP.
36. 'Chaplin Appears in Petersburg, Va.' *Moving Picture World*, 4 May 1918, p.673.
37. 'Charlie Chaplin Puts "Pep" in Crowd of 4000 People.' *Times Dispatch* [Richmond, VA], 12 April 1918, p.1.
38. 'Movie Star Will Help Sell Bonds,' *Times Dispatch* [Richmond, VA], 11 April 1918, p.1.
39. 'Rocky Mount Throngs Hear Charlie Chaplin,' *Greensboro Daily News*, 13 April 1918, p.7.
40. 'Charlie Chaplin Speaks to the People of Wilson,' *Greensboro Daily News*, 13 April 1918, p.7.
41. 'Charlie Chaplin Comes on Friday.' *News and Observer* [Raleigh, NC], 11 April 1918, p.1.
42. 'Liberty Loan Goes Beyond Halfway Point in Raleigh.' *News and Observer* [Raleigh, NC] 13 April 1918, p.1, 2.
43. 'High Point to Attend Greensboro Exercises, *Greensboro Daily News*, 10 April 1918, p.3.
44. 'Liberty Bond Parade Helped Here Greatly by Charlie Chaplin,' *Greensboro Daily News*, 14 April 1918, pp.1, 3.
45. 'Thousands Hear Chaplin Boost Liberty Bonds,' *Winston-Salem Journal*, 14 April 1918, p.7.
46. 'Charlie Chaplin Visits the County, *The Dispatch* [Lexington, NC], 17 April 1918, p.1.
47. 'Charlie Chaplin Drew Big Crowd,' *Salisbury Evening Post*, 15 April 1918, p.3.
48. 'Soldiers Greet Charlie Chaplin,' *Charlotte* [NC] *Observer*, 15 April 1918, p.2.

49. 'Chaplin Talks to Crowd of $6000 Selling $25000 of Liberty Loan.' *Charlotte* [NC] *Observer*, 15 April 1918, p.2.
50. 'Camp Jackson News: Speech Four Yards Long He Did Not Say, *The State* [Columbia, SC], 16 April 1918, p.3.
51. 'Charlie Chaplin Will Be in Columbia Monday,' *The Sunday Record* [Columbia, SC], 14 April 1918, p.19.
52. 'Vast Throng Gathers to Hear and See Chaplin,' *The Columbia Record* [SC], 15 April 1918, p.12.
53. 'Chaplin at Sumter Sells Liberty Bonds,' *The State* [Columbia, SC], 17 April 1918, p.9.
54. Don Rhodes, 'Imperial to Celebrate Charlie Chaplin's Visit to Augusta 100 Years Ago,' *August Chronicle*, 3 November 2018, https://www.augustachronicle.com/story/news/2018/11/03/imperial-to-celebrate-charlie-chaplins-visit-to-augusta-100-years-ago/9335781007/
55. 'Screen Comedian's Name Heads Roster at Red Cross Room,' *Macon Daily Telegraph*, 18 April 1918, n. p., Pressbook. CHACHAA.
56. 'Subscriptions for Bonds on Increase for Macon and Bibb,' *Macon Daily Telegraph*, 18 April 1918, p.1, 8.
57. 'Charlie Chaplin Arrives.' *The Atlanta Constitution*, 17 April 1918, p.3.
58. '8000 Buy Bonds from Charlie Chaplin.' *The Atlanta Constitution*, 18 April 1918, p.1.
59. 'Charlie Chaplin is Welcomed by Monster Crowd,' *The Tennessean* [Nashville, TN], 19 April 1918, p.1, 5.
60. 'Charlie Chaplin Here To-Morrow,' *Nashville Banner*, 17 April 1918, p.12.
61. 'Charlie Chaplin is Welcomed by Monster Crowd,' *The* Tennessean [Nashville, TN], 19 April 1918, p.5.
62. 'Movie Star in Demand.' *The Commercial Appeal* [Memphis, TN], 16 April 1918, p.5.
63. 'Memphis Bond Sales $2,668,750 to Date.' *The Commercial Appeal* [Memphis, TN], 21 April 1918, p.1, 10.
64. *The Commercial Appeal* [Memphis, TN], 21 April 1918, p.10.
65. These were, besides New Orleans, Port Arthur, Texas (24 April afternoon), Beaumont, Texas (24 April night), Galveston, Texas (25 April afternoon), Houston, Texas (25 April evening), Austin, Texas (26 April afternoon), San Antonio (26 April evening), Waco, Texas (27 April afternoon), and Dallas, Texas (27 April evening), *Official Bulletin of the United States Committee on Public Information*, 3 April 1918, n. p., Pressbook, CHACHAA. N. B. Houston, Texas was expecting Chaplin right up until 24 April when they finally received a cancellation. On 21 April, *The Houston Post*, in an article entitled 'Charlie Chaplin to Use Talents in Serving Country,' complete with photos, presented a heartfelt argument about how much effort Chaplin was making in the war effort in order to combat the bad press he was

receiving in the Northcliffe papers in Britain and how this 'new Chaplin' was 'a thinker and student of human nature and emotion, an unassuming young man who takes his business and his fame seriously' (p.39). All of this flew out the window when the cancellation occurred, however. In the same newspaper, the announcement was very brief: 'It doesn't make much difference. The old town has been rammed, jammed and crammed with celebrities so much that one does not attract attention anymore unless he marches between the Main streetcar tracks leading a star-spangled Billy goat with red whiskers.' (George M. Bailey, 'Early Morning Observations,' *The Houston Post*, 24 April 1918, p.6).

66. Another location in Louisiana, Lake Providence, had been considered, according to a 7 April mention in the *Times-Picayune* [New Orleans], p.3, but finally, not added.

67. 'New Bonds Ready Early Next Week for Cash Buyers,' *Times-Picayune* [New Orleans, LA], 21 April 1918, p.12.

68. 'Charlie Chaplin Coming Tuesday for Great Rally,' *Times-Picayune* [New Orleans, LA], 22 April 1918, p.1.

69. 'Chaplin and His Acrobatics Sell $227,000 Bonds' *Times-Picayune* [New Orleans, LA], 24 April 1918, p.1, 7.

70. 'Charlie Chaplin to Review Own Film at Strand.' *Times-Picayune* [New Orleans, LA], 21 April 1918, p.39. Worth noting is that one article says that the screening was to take place in the morning, but Chaplin didn't arrive until 2.30 pm in the afternoon. Another just states 11.00. So, the exact time of the screening is not for certain.

71. 'Chaplin and His Acrobatics Sell $227,000 Bonds,' *Times-Picayune* [New Orleans, LA], 24 April 1918, p.1, 7.

72. '$33,225,460 Daily up to City in Loan., *New York Herald*, 1 May 1918, p.5.

73. 'Rambles 'Round Filmtown,' *Moving Picture World*, 27 April 1918, p.558. It has been pointed out that although the date of this article is 27 April, it most likely was written earlier and even refers to another interview published on 10 April, when Chaplin and Fairbanks were first in New York on the tour. Since the two men had left New York on 9 April and Hill claimed to be carrying with him the article dated 10 April, his interview would have had to come during Chaplin's second appearance in New York, but perhaps a few days earlier than the 27. Also, Chaplin was reported to have been drafted by the Los Angeles board 15 April and would most likely be called to report for service in June. In fact, he was never called to serve.

74. 'Chaplin Puts 'All He Has' in Liberty Loan,' *New York Tribune*, 1 May 1918, p.9.

75. '[One of Charley Chaplin's shoes],' *New York Tribune*, 1 May 1918, p.9.

76. 'Chaplin Finishes Liberty Bond Tour,' *Moving Picture World*, 11 May 1918, p.976.

77. 'C. Chaplin is Home,' *Los Angeles Times*, 13 May 1918, p.9.

Chapter 3: World War I: *Shoulder Arms* and *The Bond*

1. Letter John Jasper, Charlie Chaplin Studios, Los Angeles to Charlie Chaplin, Memphis, Tennessee, 15 April 1918. CHACHAA.

2. Letter Syd Chaplin, Chaplin Studios, Hollywood, California, 14 October 1918 to John Jasper, 236 N. Vendome, Los Angeles, California. CHACHAA.

3. Weg, 'Charlie Chaplin, Caught Doing the Family Wash Is Found to Be Just a Wonderful Big Boy,' *St. Louis [MO] Times*, Pressbook, CHACHAA.

4. 'Chaplin Reported Injured in Pro-German Plot to Prevent Completion of Fourth Liberty Loan Film.' *New York Exhibitor's Trade Review*, 10 August 1918, n. p., Pressbook, CHACHAA.

5. 'Chaplin Release Date 8 September,' p.42.

6. Production report for 3 August 1918, *Camouflage* CHACHAA.

7. Production report for 16 August 1918, *Camouflage, Shoulder Arms* CHACHAA. Not sure why this would have been the case, because an item appeared in *Motion Picture News*, 'Chaplin film Gets Name' on 13 July 1918, p.203, more than a month before this time.

8. Production reports for 16 and 17 August 1918, *Camouflage, Shoulder Arms* CHACHAA.

9. The Daily Production Reports, Charlie Chaplin Film Co., (*The Bond*, included in the reports for *Shoulder Arms*), 16 August, 1918 – 22 August 1918 provided the dates for this section. CHACHAA.

10. Record #L12955, Library of Congress, Motion Picture Copyright Descriptions Collection, 1912–1977. LOC-MPCDC.

11. A 2-page TS in the Chaplin archives (CHACHAA) entitled simply 'Methods') does definitely state that Brown left the studios at this time. Also, he may have sold his script for *The Pest* (1919) to Goldwyn for Mabel Normand about this time. In any event, he did tell Chaplin that he was leaving for the Navy 28 September 1918, which seems unreasonably late to be just enlisting, but it's clear he never went. By July 1919, Universal hired him as a writer for comedians Lyons and Moran. He was later known for directing such films as *Buck Privates* (1928) with Zasu Pitts and the Amos and Andy series.

12. Some exhibitors were announcing a release date for the film as 26 September at this point, but First National brass would not commit to any date just yet ('[While several of the local theaters]' *Variety*, 30 August 1918, p.36).

13. The Daily Production Reports, Charlie Chaplin Film Co., (*Shoulder Arms*), 27 May 1918 – 16 September 1918 provided the dates for this section. CHACHAA. The copyright entry for this film, #L12954 shows that it was copyrighted on 8 October 1918. It contains a seven-page synopsis of the story. LOC-MPCDC.

14. '*Shoulder Arms* in Three Reels,' *Wid's Daily*, 17 September 1918, p.1.

15. Cable John Jasper Los Angeles, 3 September 1918 to Syd Chaplin aboard California Ltd. No. Two Salt Lake Line Omaha, Nebraska. CHACHAA.

16. 'Chaplin's *Shoulder Arms* in Three Reels,' *Motion Picture News*, 28 September 1918, p.2022.

17. 'Producers Agree on Complete Shutdown: No New Films or Reissues for One Month,' *Exhibitors Herald*, 26 October 1918, p.21.

18. 'Statement Made Regarding *Shoulder Arms*,' *Motion Picture News*, 26 October 1918, n. p, CHACHAA.

19. 'Chaplin First at Strand,' *Variety*, 27 September 1918, p.50.

20. '*Shoulder Arms* Has October 20 Showing,' *Motion Picture News*, 19 October 1918, p.2570.

21. 'Story of *Shoulder Arms* Proves Difficult to Produce,' *Montgomery Alabama Advertiser*, 24 November 1918, n. p., CHACHAA.

22. 'Chaplin Held Over,' *Variety*, 25 October 1918, p.39 and 'Extra Week for Chaplin at Strand Theatre,' *Motion Picture News*, 9 November 1918, p.2865. The Broadway Theatre in New York extended the film to three weeks and an extension from three days to a full week for all the vaudeville houses in the B F. Keith circuit (meaning many other already-booked acts had to be cut) indicated the film would be a greater success than any other Chaplin film to date ('*Shoulder Arms* Three Weeks at Broadway,' *Motion Picture News*, 23 November 1918, p.3082).

23. 'Charlie Chaplin, Playing a Soldier, Keeps Them All Roaring in *Shoulder Arms*,' *New York Review*, 24 October 1918, n. p., CHACHAA.

24. 'What They Do in Seattle,' *Motion Picture News*, 28 December 1918, p.3948.

25. 'Tally to Build Another Theatre,' *Motion Picture News*, 21 December 1918, p.3711.

26. Quoted directly from Chaplin's complaint in 'Chaplin Sues to Protect His Inimitable Antics,' *Moving Picture World*, 23 November 1918, p.816.

27. 'Chaplin Sues Promoters of Alleged Imitator,' *Motion Picture News*, 30 November 1918, p.3199.

28. Loeb consulted his lawyer, Mortimer Hays, directly after seeing the film for the first time, 5 October 1921, with his suit making the papers on 30 October 1921. Depositions for the trial had been taken in 1924 and an initial action had been overseen by Judge Knox in 1926, which resulted simply in the suit being moved to trial court instead of equity court. At this point Nathan Burkan took over as attorney from Lloyd Wright, who had been handling it previously. Burkan had the case moved to the Federal District Court of New York, given that Chaplin was not an American citizen.

29. Lita Grey Chaplin had filed for divorce 10 January 1927 and Chaplin had responded 2 June 1927. This 'plagiarism' court case fell nicely in between.

30. Leo Loeb v. Charles Chaplin, 4 May – 15 May 1927, stenographer's minutes (Day 1, plaintiff opening statement). CHACHAA.
31. Leo Loeb v. Charles Chaplin, 4 May – 15 May 1927, stenographer's minutes (Day 2, defense cross-examination of Loeb). CHACHAA.
32. The Plaintiff's attorney Hays refused to have the actual film shown to the jury for comparison.
33. Leo Loeb v. Charles Chaplin, 4 May – 15 May 1927, stenographer's minutes (Day 3, defense cross-examination of Loeb). CHACHAA.
34. 'Chaplin Suit Goes to Jury,' *Express* 11 May 1927, n p., Pressbook. CHACHAA.
35. 'Jury Discharged,' *The Daily Item* [Port Chester, NY], 12 May 1927, p.15.
36. Also mentioned in the suit tangentially was the fact that there already existed several different versions of *Shoulder Arms* by 1927, due to censorship after the war. Project MASh, directed by Adrien Gerber of the Kinemathek Bern, is a recent attempt to collect these different versions of the film, beginning in spring 2021 and ending 18 months later. It has been established that Chaplin himself constructed four authorized prints of the film, which, for one reason or another, were altered over the years. Information on the films included in the project so far and Gerber's overall history of the film's incarnations can be found on the project's dedicated site at https://lichtspiel.ch/en/mash/?fbclid=IwAR0kyJWX6u3Ph17lDI_0__ w3RE3d0oxKIqH7LEDqFp6RNkBQhrseeKoyccc. Gerber also has an article on the topic: 'Camera Negatives, Releases, and Versions of Chaplin's *Shoulder Arms* (1918),' *Early Popular Visual Culture*, 19/1 (2021), p.38-51. Also, beyond this effort, there are other scholars and film afficionados investigating multiple prints of not just the First National Films but Chaplin films from other periods as well.
37. An article entitled ' "Not engaged"– C. Chaplin' *Los Angeles Times*, 25 July 1918, p.11 mentioned that rumors abounded that Chaplin and Mildred Harris were engaged, being that Mildred sported a beautiful diamond ring and that the 'two are seen together almost constantly.' Both denied this.
38. December 1918, p.186–192.
39. 'Chaplin, Film Star, Weds Sub Rosa.' *Los Angeles Evening Express*, 9 November 1918, p.5.

Chapter 4: A Period of Stagnation: Life with Mildred Harris and Severe Creative Blockage: *Sunnyside* (1919), *A Day's Pleasure* (1919) and the formation of United Artists

1. Emma Lindsay Squier, 'The Sad Business of Being Funny,' *Motion Picture*, April 1919, p.46.
2. See 'Chaplin's Comedy for First National Nears Completion,' *Exhibitor's Herald*, 16 March 1918, p.21 or 'Screen Gossip: [Charlie Chaplin has chosen],' *Picture-Play*, June 1918, p.297.

3. 'Chaplin's Pictures,' *Wid's Daily*, 16 January 1919, p.1.

4. 'Charlie Chaplin Ill; Will Close Studio,' *Los Angeles Evening Herald*, 13 January 1919, p.1.

5. Hart was later to remove his support.

6. See my book, *Syd Chaplin: A Biography*, Jefferson, NC: McFarland & Co., 2010, p.80-81, also A.H. Giebler, 'Rubbernecking in Filmland,' *Moving Picture World*, 1 February 1919, p.607-608, and, also, Tino Balio, *United Artists: The Company Built by the Stars*, Madison, WI: U of Wisconsin P, 1976, p.12–13.

7. A.H. Giebler, 'Rubbernecking in Filmland,' *Moving Picture World*, 1 February 1919, p.607-608.

8. Chaplin's return to the studio wasn't announced to the press until 15 February ('Chaplin Gives up Plan to Go to Europe,' *New York Review*, 2 February 1919, n. p., Pressbook, CHACHAA).

9. J.D. Williams, 'First National's Manager Replies to Zukor's Query,' *Wid's Daily*, 1 December 1918, p.7, 9, 31.

10. 'Statement of Chaplin's Policy,' *Motion Picture News*, 5 October, 1918, p.2193. Also, 'Chaplin Makes Statement of Policy,' *Moving Picture World*, 5 October 1918, p.64.

11. Cable J.D. Williams, New York to Charles Chaplin, Los Angeles, 3 February 1919. CHACHAA.

12. TS J.D. Williams, New York to Charles Chaplin, Los Angeles, 10 February 1919. CHACHAA.

13. TS J.D. Williams, New York to Charles Chaplin, Los Angeles, 10 February 1919. CHACHAA.

14. TS J.D. Williams, New York to Charles Chaplin, Los Angeles, 10 February 1919. CHACHAA.

15. Tino Balio, *United Artists: The Company Built by the Stars*, Madison, WI: U of WI P, 1976, 24-27.

16. 'Williams Hits out from Shoulder.' *Moving Picture World*, 22 February 1919, p.1009.

17. Tino Balio, *United Artists: The Company Built by the Stars*, Madison, WI: U of WI P, 1976, p.29.

18. Tino Balio, *United Artists: The Company Built by the Stars*, Madison, WI: U of WI P, 1976, p.34-35.

19. While the 5 March 1919 letter granting this request doesn't exist, it is referenced in a letter dated 20 May 1920 from Harry Schwalbe in New York to Charles Chaplin in Los Angeles. CHACHAA.

20. See my book *Syd Chaplin: A Biography*, Jefferson, NC: McFarland & Co., 2010 for the whole story.

21. Graham, Cooper C. and Christoph Irmscher, eds. *Love and Loss in Hollywood: Florence Deshon, Max Eastman and Charlie Chaplin*. Bloomington, IN: Indiana UP, 2021, p.92-95, 197-200.

22. TS John Fairbanks, Los Angeles to J.D. Williams, New York, 11 March 1919. CHACHAA.
23. Letter Harry Schwalbe, First National, New York City, 5 March 1919, to Arthur Wright, Currier Bldg., Los Angeles, CHACHAA.
24. 'Wind and Snow in Storm Wake,' *Los Angeles Times*, 15 March 1919, p.13.
25. '*Sunnyside* is Chaplin's Next First National Release,' *Moving Picture World*, 9 March 1919, n.p .Pressbook, CHACHAA.
26. David Robinson's filmography lists this actor as Tom Teriss, but Park Jones is noted throughout the production notes as the actor playing this specific part.
27. Elsie Codd, 'The Crucible of Creation,' *Shadow Stage*, October-November 1919, p.15.
28. The Daily Production Reports, Charlie Chaplin Film Co., (*Sunnyside*), 4 November 1918 – 15 April 1919 were used to discern dates in this section. CHACHAA. The copyright entry #L13780 shows that copyright was granted 4 June 1919 and includes a one-page synopsis. LOC-MPCDC.
29. 'Failure of Chaplin *Sunnyside* Causes Upheaval in Filmdom,' *Variety*, 4 July 1919, n. p., Pressbook, CHACHAA.
30. Letter Harry Schwalbe, First National, New York, 20 November 1919, to Arthur Wright, Currier Bldg, Los Angeles. CHACHAA.
31. '*Sunnyside* Is Unique Among Chaplin's Films,' *New York Mail*, 16 June 1919, n. p., Pressbook, CHACHAA.
32. 'Charlie Chaplin Screened in His Latest Comedy,' *Charleston* [SC] *News-Courier*, 26 June 1919, n. p., Pressbook, CHACHAA.
33. Review of *Sunnyside*, *Motion Picture News*, 28 June 1919, n. p., Pressbook, CHACHAA.
34. '*Sunnyside* Breaks Records at Detroit,' *Exhibitors Herald*, 26 July 1919, n. p., Pressbook, CHACHAA.
35. '*Sunnyside's* Failure Hands Charlie Chaplin Real Laugh,' *Variety*, 18 July 1919, n. p., Pressbook, CHACHAA.
36. Elsie Codd, 'Charlie Chaplin in *A Day's Pleasure*,' *Pictures and Picturegoer*, 13 March 1920, p.261.
37. Shooting Schedule for *A Day's Pleasure*, 30 June to 9 July 1919, CHACHAA.
38. Many lengthy condolence articles appeared in the British press at the time of the child's death. Perhaps Elsie Codd's is the most moving: 'It was only a few weeks ago that I started work on that little frock, and yet now it seems as though years had passed since I began that labor of love, sewing into each white stitch all the tender thoughts that every woman dreams over the tiny garments of a little child. And now I have put it away in a little soft nest, sweet with the scent of lavender, but often I shall take it out and look at it and remember the day when with tear-dimmed eyes I laid it away with all the hope and ambitions of two sorrowing parents.' ('In Memoriam,' *Pictures and the Picturegoer*, 30 August 1919, n. p. Pressbook, CHACHAA.

39. As mentioned before, it is more likely that Chaplin had been considering a child co-star for some time before his son's death, but this event may have been the catalyst he needed.

40. This is noted on Production report for *The Ford Story*, 7 October 1919, CHACHAA.

41. The Daily Production Reports, Charlie Chaplin Film Co., (*A Day's Pleasure*), 21 May 1919 – 19 October 1919 provided dates for this section. CHACHAA. The copyright entry for this film, #LL14469 is dated 26 November 1919 and includes a two-page synopsis and cast of characters. LOC-MPCDC.

42. 'First National Gets New Chaplin Comedy *A Day's Pleasure*,' *Motion Picture News*, 29 November 1919, p.3947.

43. 'The Strand,' *Variety*, 12 December 1919, p.45.

44. 'Editorial Calls Chaplin Real National Asset,' *Motion Picture News*, 17 January 1920, p.864.

Chapter 5: Betting on *The Kid* (1921): The First Feature Comedy with both a 'Laughter and a Tear'

1. J.D. Williams, 'The Coming Revolution in Filmland,' *Motion Picture News*, 13 December 1919, p.4295.

2. As related by Rollie Totheroh in Timothy J. Lyons, ed., 'Roland H. Totheroh Interviewed,' *Film Culture* (Spring 1972), p.266.

3. Albert Austin, a former Karno colleague of Chaplin's, went on to try his hand at directing, being touted as Jackie Coogan's sole director as of 6 January 1922 ('Albert Austin to Direct,' *Los Angeles Times*, 6 January 1922, p.32). His directing career was limited to ten films, only two of which were with Coogan. He would also direct Chaplin's child star from *The Pilgrim*, Dean Riesner, in his only starring vehicle, *Prince of a King* (1923). Austin appears with Chaplin again, however, as an actor in *City Lights* (1931).

4. '[Because Charles Chaplin]', *Santa Ana* [CA] *Register*, 18 February 1920, n. p., Pressbook, CHACHAA.

5. 'Romance and a Honeymoon,' *Los Angeles Times*, 12 February 1922 p.53.

6. 'Boys Will Be Boys,' *Los Angeles Evening Express*, 25 February 1922, p.22. For more about Linder and Chaplin, see my book *The Rise and Fall of Max Linder: Cinema's First Celebrity*, Orlando, FL: BearManor Media, 2021.

7. 'Chaplin in Fist Fight,' *Los Angeles Times*, 8 April 1920, pp.1, 7.

8. Timothy J. Lyons, ed., 'Roland H. Totheroh Interviewed,' *Film Culture* (Spring 1972), p.266.

9. 'Chaplin's Feet on Job Again,' *Los Angeles Times*, 9 April 1920, p.15.

10. Cable Charlie Chaplin, Los Angeles to Syd Chaplin, Hotel Claridge, New York City, 9 April 1920. CHACHAA.

11. See Cable Charlie Chaplin, Los Angeles to Syd Chaplin, Hotel Claridge, New York City, 14 April 1920. CHACHAA and Cable Tom Harrington,

Los Angeles to Syd Chaplin, Hotel Claridge, New York City, 15 April 1920. CHACHAA.

12. Letter Harry Schwalbe, New York to Charles Chaplin, Los Angeles, 20 May 1920. CHACHAA.

13. J.M. Barrie is the author of *Peter Pan*.

14. Grace Kingsley, 'The Kid Reigns,' *Los Angeles Times*, 21 February 1921, p.21.

15. The Daily Production Reports, Charlie Chaplin Film Co. (*The Kid*), 21 May 1919 – 31 July 1920 were used to discern dates during the production. CHACHAA.

16. 'Chaplin's Wife Asks Divorce,' *Los Angeles Times*, 3 August 1920, p.13.

17. Timothy J. Lyons, ed., 'Roland H. Totheroh Interviewed,' *Film Culture* (spring 1972), p.267.

18. 'Film Comedian Cornered Here,' *Salt Lake City* [UT] *Tribune*, 9 August 1920, p.14.

19. 'Chaplin Will Finish Big Film Here; Says Divorce Case Is Due to Lawyers,' *Deseret News* [Salt Lake City, UT], 11 August 1920, p.9.

20. 'Comedian Balks Process Servers by Visit to S. L.,' *Salt Lake* [UT] *Telegram*, 11 August 1920, p.2.

21. Production of *The Kid* took only one year.

22. 'Another Chaplin Comes; Doug and Mary Visit S. L.,' *Salt Lake* [UT] *Telegram*, 13 August 1920, p.2.

23. pp.267-8.

24. As Totheroh noted in his interview, David Horsley was truly one of the pioneers of the American film industry. Born in northern England, Horsley moved his family to Bayonne, New Jersey, in 1884 where he formed the Centaur Film Company with his brother William and former Biograph employee Chester Gorman in 1907. By 1910 they were producing three films a week, including the *Mutt and Jeff* comedies. In 1911, they moved the studio to California, changed its name to the Nestor and moved into a building on the corner of Sunset and Gower, thereby becoming the first motion picture studio in Hollywood. Just a year later, the Horsley Brothers threw in with several other independent film companies, including Carl Laemmle's Independent to form Universal, but the merger was not a happy one. Horsley sold out to Laemmle just a year later, but Nestor's original property became Universal Studios proper thereafter. By 1920, when Totheroh and Wilson came knocking, Horsley had sold off his studio building on E Street in Bayonne (it burned down anyway in 1917), but still owned his brother's renowned laboratory at 900 Broadway, which doubled as the company offices back in the day. It was this building that served as the maternity ward for Chaplin's still vestigial film. See Kathleen M. Middleton, *Bayonne*, Charleston, SC: Arcadia Publishing, 1995, p.94.

25. p.268.

26. p.268.
27. *Exhibitors Herald*, 4 September 1920, p.47.
28. In addition to appearing in the local press, this interview also appeared in *Pictures Press*, 21 August 1920, entitled 'Chapin Issues Defiance' by Stephen J. Moloney, p.17.
29. 'First National Takes Issue with Charlie Chaplin,' *Motion Picture News*, 4 September 1920, p.1853.
30. Cable M. Gilbert, New York to S. Gilbert, Hotel Utah, Salt Lake City, 3 September 1920. CHACHAA. Gilbert was Minnie Chaplin's (Syd's wife's) maiden name.
31. 'Chaplin Here,' *Wid's Daily*, 11 September 1920, p.1.
32. 'Chaplin Makes Dash for East,' *Los Angeles Times*, 27 August 1920, p.13.
33. 'Mildred Harris to Drop Los Angeles Action; May Ask for a Receiver,' *Los Angeles Times*, 13 September 1920, p.17.
34. 'Mrs. Chaplin's Goal Now Gold,' *Los Angeles Times*, 15 September 1920, p.17.
35. 'Chaplin Rents Plant,' *Los Angeles Times*, 8 October 1920, p.32.
36. 'Chaplin to Return Here and Get Busy,' *Los Angeles Times*, 10 October 1920, p.1.
37. '[Our sympathy],' *The Whittier News* [CA], 27 October 1920, p.2.
38. 'Mildred Harris (Not Chaplin) Has Ambitions,' *Los Angeles Evening Express*, 6 November 1920, p.34.
39. 'Mildred Harris Chaplin Gets Divorce and Cash,' *Los Angeles Times*, 13 November 1920, p.15.
40. Lyons, 'Roland H. Totheroh Interviewed,' p.268.
41. Amended Agreement, Associated First National Pictures, Co. with Chaplin for *The Kid*, 3 December 1920. CHACHAA. The copyright entry for the film, #L16019, includes a two-page synopsis and cast of characters. It was granted on 17 January 1921. LOC-MPCDC.
42. This claim is made in articles such as 'First National Franchise-Holders Convene at Chicago,' *Motion Picture News*, 22 January 1921, p.826, 'Release of *The Kid* Settled,' *Motion Picture News*, 13 January 1921, p.717, and it is even mentioned on a full-page ad for the film in *Exhibitors Herald*, 26 February 1921, p.30.
43. First National ad for *The Kid*, *Exhibitors Herald*, 26 February 1921, p.30.
44. Quoted in 'Charlie Chaplin's *The Kid* in Chicago,' *Exhibitors Herald*, 29 January 1921, p.56.
45. Quoted in First National ad for *The Kid*, *Exhibitors Herald*, 26 February 1921, p.30.
46. '*The Kid* Reigns,' *Los Angeles Times*, 21 February 1921, p.21.

Chapter 6: Back to Work in Hollywood: Filming *The Idle Class*

 1. See 'Chaplin Back in LA,' *Long Beach* [CA] *Telegram*, 9 December 1920, p.1 or 'Girls, Charlie Is Back and Single,' *Evening Vanguard* [Venice, CA], 10 December 1920, p.5 as examples.
 2. 'Chaplin Ready to Start,' *Los Angeles Times*, 17 December 1920, p.32.
 3. United Artists Corporate minutes for 6 December 1920 indicate that Mack Sennett first approached Doug Fairbanks about a possible merger of the two organizations.
 4. 'Combine Imminent,' *Los Angeles Times*, 7 January 1921, p.30.
 5. 'Abrams Declares Merger of Big Four and A. P.'s Off,'" *Exhibitors Herald*, 29 January 1921, p.39.
 6. 'Not a Moving Picture,' *Whittier* [CA] *News*, 1 March 1921, p.8.
 7. 'First National Explains its Attitude on *The Kid*,' *Exhibitors Herald*, 26 February 1921, p.37.
 8. Aubrey Chaplin's film industry aspirations never came to fruition.
 9. Cable Charlie Chaplin, Los Angeles to Syd Chaplin, New York, 21 April 1919. CHACHAA.
10. 'Mrs. Chaplin Arrives,' *Los Angeles Evening Post-Record*, 4 April 1921, p.5.
11. For more detailed information on this story, see Chapter 5 in my *Syd Chaplin: A Biography*.
12. This location over Griffith Park was ascertained by articles such as 'Several Affairs at Pasadena Golf Club,' *The Pasadena* [CA] *Post*, 9 March 1921, p.8.
13. 'When Film Comedian Meets Executive,' *Los Angeles Evening Express*, 11 March 1921, p.26.
14. 'Film Combine Head Leaves for East,' *Los Angeles Times*, 19 March 1921, p.21.
15. 'Chaplin Will Shuffle to Altar,' *Pasadena* [CA] *Post*, 7 April 1921, p.1.
16. 'Chaplin Will See May Collins Act,' *Los Angeles Times*, 15 April 1921, p.32.
17. Grace Kingsley, 'May Collins with U.,' *Los Angeles Times*, 30 April 1921, p.31.
18. 'Charlie Chaplin Born 32 Years Ago Today,' *Los Angeles Evening Express*, 16 April 1921, p.15.
19. 'Gossip of Screen and Stage,' *Los Angeles Evening Express*, 22 April 1921, p 30.
20. 'Heavyweight with Chaplin,' *Los Angeles Times*, 22 April 1921, p.48.
21. 'Chaplin Is Sued for Heavy Attorney Fee,' *Los Angeles Times*, 30 April 1921, p.5.
22. 'Verdict Sealed in Chaplin Case,' *Salt Lake* [UT] *Tribune*, 3 May 1922, p.22.
23. 'Jury Awards $4000 Fee in Chaplin Case,' *Deseret News* [Salt Lake City, UT], 3 May 1922, p.11.
24. The press reported this as occurring on 10 May, but the production reports don't jive with that date. The accident must have occurred 4 May. 'Asbestos B. V. D.'s Save Chaplin Bad Burns,' *Pasadena* [CA] *Post*, 11 May 1921, p.3.

25. 'Harry Maynard with Chaplin,' *Los Angeles Times*, 11 March 1921, p.34.

26. 'Everybody's Ill, Shucks!' *Los Angeles Evening Post-Record*, 11 June 1921, p.16.

27. 'Chaplin's Life Threatened; Man Jailed in North,' *Los Angeles Times*, 23 June 1921, p.20.

28. Calculations for the 1921 apparition of the comet suggested that it would collide with the Earth in June of that year, but observations made on 10 April ruled out any impact.

29. A 29 April 1922 article entitled 'Hollywood Hit by Radio Craze,' in the *Los Angeles Evening Citizen News* noted that Garcia was a pioneer in the radio industry, having taken up the obsession in 1906 in San Francisco: 'Together with Dr. Lee Forest, another radio authority, he experimented with the radiophone, and in 1903 and 1904 succeeded in transmitting and receiving wireless phone messages for a distance of one half mile along the beach, and with an aerial stretched between the Palace and Grand hotels, established one of the first complete wireless telegraph stations in the country' (p.8). Chaplin was always surrounding himself with talented people!

30. 'Charlie Chaplin to Play Dual Role,' *Los Angeles Evening Express*, 17 June 1921, p.30 and Grace Kingsley, 'Chaplin Doubles,' *Los Angeles Times*, 15 June 1921, p.36.

31. The Daily Production Reports, Charlie Chaplin Film Co. (*The Idle Class*), 29 January 1921 – 24 June 1921 have been used to determine dates in this section. CHACHAA. The copyright entry for this film, #L16934, showed that the copyright was granted 14 September 1921 and included a one-page synopsis and cast list. LOC-MPCDC.

32. 'Chaplin Changes Title of New Picture,' 15 July 1921, press clipping. CHACHAA.

33. 'Crowds Storm Strand to See Chaplin Film,' *San Francisco* [CA] *Call*, 7 November 1921, n. p., Pressbook, CHACHAA.

34. 'Even Dressed Up, Chaplin Draws Crowds,' *Los Angeles Times*, 6 November 1921, p.62.

35. '*Serenade* Romantic Film Play at Kinema,' *Los Angeles Times*, 7 November 1921, p.26.

36. '*Idle Class* Zippy,' *Los Angeles Times*, 31 October 1921, p.26.

37. First National ad for *The Idle Class*, *Motion Picture News*, 22 October 1921, p.2134.

38. 'Chaplin Increase,' *Variety*, 19 August 1921, p.33.

39. Contract between Charles Chaplin and First National Exhibitors' Circuit regarding *The Idle Class*, dated 31 October 1921. CHACHAA.

40. '120 *Idle Class* Prints,' *Variety*, 14 October 1921, p 46.

41. 'Resolutions Adopted by Minnesota and Eastern Pennsylvania Organizations,' *Exhibitors Trade Review*, 5 November 1921, p.1568.

42. 'New Charlie Chaplin Film,' *Evening Standard*, 19 September 1921, n. p., Pressbook, CHACHAA.
43. 'Charlie Chapin in *The Idle Class*,' *The Daily Mail*, 24 October 1921, n. p., Pressbook, CHACHAA.
44. A plaque existing at the house today dates Chaplin's residence to 23 April 1921.
45. Theosophy was founded in 1875 by Madame Blavatsky, H.S. Olcott and others in New York City. The Hollywood colony lasted only from 1912 to 1926, when it moved headquarters to Ojai, California. A famous American devotée, Annie Besant, took up residence in the Krotona Colony of Hollywood in July 1918. Many of the Krotona buildings have been either restored, repurposed or both, but are in existence still today. See Alfred Willis, 'A Survey of Surviving Buildings of the Krotona Colony in Hollywood,' *Architronic*, 8 (1), 1998: 1–18.
46. Jacqueline Shannon, 'Mega Lifestyle: Moorcrest,' 2021, *megadreamshomes. com*. Available at http://www.megadreamhomes.com/megalifestyles/moorcrest/default.htm.
47. '[For Sale: Beautiful Hillside Corner Lot],' *Los Angeles Times*, 7 June 1921, p.16.

Chapter 7: *The Kid* Reception in Britain and Chaplin's Homecoming Tour (September–October 1921)

1. Harris's testimony included Chaplin's mistreatment of her on their first Christmas together when Harris had just been released from the hospital after treatment for a nervous condition. Chaplin failed to come home on Christmas Eve, after he had told her 'he would be home and have dinner with me and help me trim the Christmas tree' ('What Charlie,' n. p.). When he did arrive home in the early hours of the morning, he woke Harris up to castigate her for buying so many presents. On Christmas day, he arose very late and continued to yell at her for her overindulgence, stating that 'he did not believe in such things' ('What Charlie,' n. p.). Such pronouncements must have seemed sacrilegious to working-class Americans.

2. Gehring, in his book *Charlie Chaplin and A Woman of Paris* (McFarland 2021) points to a telling passage in "Charles Chaplin Is Too Tragic to Play Hamlet,' *Stanly* [Albemarle, NC] *News-Herald*, 11 February 1921, p.6, which turns out to be excerpted from a *Current Opinion* article of the same title, published February 1921, pp.187–188, and which Gehring dates February 1922, 'I once had a day vision. I saw at my feet in a huddled heap all the trappings and paraphernalia of my screen clothes – that dreadful suit of clothes – my mustache, the battered derby, the little cane, the broken shoes, the dirty collar. I felt as though my body had fallen from me and that I was leaving behind an eternal seeming for a vast reality. That day I resolved

never to get into those clothes again – to retire to some Italian lake with my beloved violin, my Shelley and Keats, and live under an assumed name a life purely imaginative and intellectual.' The quote has been corrected here from Gehring's alterations and so seems less an expression of hate and disgust than simply of ennui. As is known, Chaplin continued to play the Little Tramp in four more feature films following his First National contract.

3. See David Robinson's *Chaplin: His Life and Art*, (1985, 2001), p.255, *Chaplin: The Mirror of Opinion*, page 63, and Charles Maland's *Chaplin and American Culture: The Evolution of a Star Image*, Princeton, NJ: Princeton UP (1989), pp.55-6.

4. *My Trip Abroad* (1922), p.1.

5. *MTA*, p.7.

6. *MTA* p.17.

7. 'Charlie Chaplin's *My Trip Abroad*,' n. p., Pressbook, CHACHAA.

8. *MTA*, p.87.

9. *MTA*, p.98.

10. *MTA*, p.101.

11. *MTA*, p.26.

12. *MTA*, p.92.

13. 'Chaplin Entertains Fifty "Young Visitors" at the Ritz,' *Glasgow Bulletin*, 19 September 1921, n. p., Pressbook CHACHAA.

14. 'Parisians Chase Charlie to Hotel,' *The Morning Telegraph*, 18 September, 1921, n. p., Pressbook, CHACHAA.

15. Under the umbrella of S. Instone & Company, Ltd., Instone Airline operated out of the Croydon Airport outside London from 1920 to 1924. The only route available to the public during Chaplin's visit was the London to Paris route, which was then discontinued in 1922 due to competition. The airline was absorbed into Imperial Airways on 1 April 1924. See Alfred Instone, *Early Birds: Air Transport Memories, 1919–1924*, Cardiff, Wales: *Western Mail & Echo*, 1938 for more information.

16. 'Film Stars in Paris,' *Pall Mall & Globe*, 6 October 1921, n. p., Pressbook, CHACHAA.

17. Pascal Bastin, 'Au Trocadero: "Le Gosse,"' *Le Merle Blanc*, 24 September 1921, n. p., Pressbook, CHACHAA. Translation from the French by the author.

18. 'Charlie's Spurt to Go Home,' *Sunday Chronicle*, 9 October 1921, n. p., Pressbook, CHACHAA.

19. *MTA* was released to the public less than five months after Chaplin returned from his tour in October 1921.

20. Monta Bell was an experienced journalist at the time of ghostwriting *MTA* (he was editor-in-chief of *The Washington Herald*). In fact, if composition

time is any indication, it is interesting to note that Dickens, arriving back in England in June of 1842 would have taken approximately five months to complete *American Notes* by the time it appeared in November of that year and Bell also completed *MTA* in five months (Chaplin's tour ended in October 1921 and the book appeared in February 1922).

21. 'Charlie's Unhappy Week,' *Los Angeles Evening Express*, 28 January 1922, p.10.
22. 'Chaplin Revives Ancient Custom,' *Pomona* [CA] *Progress Bulletin*, 29 April 1922, p.10.
23. The Daily Production Reports, Charlie Chaplin Film Co. (*Pay Day*), 6 August 1921 – 23 February 1922 were used to define dates in this section. CHACHAA.
24. It was announced completed to the press on 11 February ('Chaplin Finishes,' *Los Angeles Times*, p.26)
25. The copyright for this film, #L17635, was granted on 13 March 1922 and included a one-page synopsis and cast list. LOC-MPCDC.
26. 'Chaplin Subject Completed,' *Motion Picture News*, 4 March, 1922, p.1401.
27. 'Chaplin Pays to See Latest', *Tacoma* [WA] *News*, 1 April 1922, n. p.
28. 'Comedian Must Be a Tragedian Also,' *Los Angeles Times*, 16 April 1922, p.56.
29. 'On the Screen,' *New York Tribune*, 3 April 1922, p.8.
30. 'Some Rarely Funny Scenes in Latest Chaplin Picture,' *New York Herald*, 3 April 1922, p.8.
31. However, Deshon's brother Walter searched assiduously for the gold cigarette case Chaplin was supposed to have given Deshon, to no avail.
32. See the following: 'Clews [*sic*] Sought in Death Case,' *Los Angeles Times*, 6 February 1922, pp.15, 20, 'Max Eastman Denies Actress Killed Self Because of Quarrel,' *Daily News* [NY, NY], 6 February 1922, p.27, 'Miss Deshon Buried,' *Los Angeles Times*, 7 February 1922, p.2, and 'Max Eastman Gives Blood for Actress,' *New York Herald*, 6 February 1922, p.7.
33. 'Screen: The Clown a Poet,' *New York Times*, 19 March 1922, p.106.
34. Grace Kingsley, 'Chaplin Dances,' *Los Angeles Times*, 11 March 1922, p.29.
35. Grace Kingsley, 'Luck Lies in Star's "Kisses,"' *Los Angeles Times*, 6 March 1922, p.15. Also, Edwin Schallert, 'Chaplin and the Ladies,' *Picture-Play*, August 1922, p.16–19, 103–104.
36. 'Busy Days Ahead for "Charlie," The Custard Pie Man,' *News-Pilot* [San Pedro, CA], 8 March 1922, p.5.
37. '"Charlie Aplin" Says Chaplin Is Jealous and Not Original,' *Los Angeles Evening Express*, 9 March 1922, p.8.
38. 'Charles Chaplin, Plaintiff, vs. Western Feature Productions, Superior Court of the State of California.' CHACHAA.

Chapter 8: Finishing Up the Contract: *The Pilgrim* (1923) and Its Controversies

1. Noted in pencil on a page of a document entitled 'Title Suggestions.' CHACHAA.
2. Robinson, *Chaplin: His Life and Art*, pp.310–311.
3. 'Story and Continuity Notes/*The Pilgrim*.' CHACHAA. Interestingly, the vamp scene is included on each draft of the story notes, so must have been deleted late in production.
4. 'Church News,' newspaper prop from *The Pilgrim*, 1922. CHACHAA.
5. The term 'faction' was used to mean 'scenes,' 'sections,' or 'sequences of film' and was used at least in the Chaplin studios and the Harold Lloyd productions. Chaplin and company had been using the term at least since the Mutual period. Lloyd reported that the term signified 'a sequence within a picture – any set of incidents turning on a common theme or locale' (Qtd. in Fred Goodwins, *Charlie Chaplin's Red Letter Days: At Work with the Comic Genius*, ed. David James, Lanham, MD: Rowman & Littlefield, 2017, p.313).
6. 'New Releasing Plan Arranged,' *Los Angeles Evening Citizen News*, 21 April 1922, p.5.
7. Story related by 'Dinkie' Dean Riesner at a Chaplin UK Society meeting in London, May 2001.
8. 'Charlie Chaplin Has New Protegé,' *Motion Picture News*, February 27, 1923, p.852. Dean Riesner acted in only five silent films as a child actor, and only one of those was in a starring role, *A Prince of a King* (1923), in which he played Gigi, the Prince. The director was Chaplin stalwart Albert Austin. However, Riesner's true calling in the business was writing screenplays, which he did beginning in 1939 with the film *Code of the Secret Service*. He wrote for both films and television, being best known as the writer of the Clint Eastwood's *Dirty Harry* franchise.
9. Daily Production reports for *The Tail End* (*The Pilgrim*), 2 April 1922 – 15 July 1922 have been consulted throughout this section. CHACHAA. The copyright for this film, #L18607, was granted on 24 January 1923 and contained a one-page synopsis and cast list. LOC-MPCDC.
10. 'Mountbattens Say Grand Canyon Is Greatest Wonder Found on Six Weeks' Tour of America,' *Courier-Journal [Louisville, KY]*, 26 November 1922, p.6.
11. Cable Charlie Chaplin, Los Angeles, California to Lord and Lady Louis Mountbatten, Metropolitan Club, Washington, D.C., 24 October 1922. CHACHAA.
12. Letter Lord 'Dickie' Mountbatten, Broadlands, Romsey, Hampshire, UK to Charlie Chaplin, Vevey, Switzerland, 13 December 1965. CHACHAA
13. Cable Charlie Chaplin, Los Angeles to Nathan Burkan, New York City, 25 September 1922. CHACHAA.

14. *The Professor* in two reels synopsis. 1922. CHACHAA.
15. 'Charlie Chaplin Here Planning for Pictures,' *San Francisco Chronicle*, November 7, 1922, p.10.
16. 'Chaplin Here but Fades from Sight,' *San Francisco Examiner*, November 7, 1922, p.7.
17. 'Engaged? Charlie Chaplin Says "Nay, Nay," But Famous Film Star Talks of Women,' *San Francisco Chronicle*, 9 November 1922, p.13.
18. *Variety* noted the pair's arrival in New York at the Biltmore on 17 November 1922. Arthur Kelly was the brother of Hetty Kelly, Chaplin's first love.
19. Cable Sydney Chaplin, New York to Charlie Chaplin, Los Angeles, 13 November 1922. CHACHAA.
20. Cable Charlie Chaplin, Los Angeles to Syd Chaplin, New York, 14 November 1922. CHACHAA.
21. Cable Syd Chaplin, New York to Charlie Chaplin, Los Angeles, 20 November 1922. CHACHAA.
22. Cable Charlie Chaplin, Los Angeles to Syd Chaplin, New York, 21 November 1922. CHACHAA.
23. 'Chaplin Parades in Chaplain Clothes in His New Film,' *Vancouver* [BC, Canada] *Daily World*, 30 November 1922, p.6.
24. Cable Charlie Chaplin, Los Angeles to Sydney Chaplin (Snyder Chaplain), New York, 6 December 1922. CHACHAA.
25. Cable Alf Reeves, Los Angeles to Syd Chaplin, New York, 6 December 1922. CHACHAA.
26. Cable Charlie Chaplin, Los Angeles to Syd Chaplin, New York, 7 December 1922. CHACHAA.
27. Cable Charlie Chaplin, Los Angeles to Syd Chaplin, New York, 15 December 1922. CHACHAA.
28. Cable Alf Reeves, Los Angeles to Syd Chaplin, New York, 20 December 1922. CHACHAA.
29. Cable Alf Reeves, Los Angeles to Syd Chaplin, New York, 21 December 1922. CHACHAA.
30. Cable Charlie Chaplin, Los Angeles to Syd Chaplin, New York, 22 December 1922. CHACHAA.
31. 'Original Contract *The Pilgrim* and *Pay Day*,'9 January 1923. CHACHAA.
32. '*The Pilgrim* Goes to First National,' *Motion Picture News*, 20 January 1923, p.298.
33. 'Same Old Charlie Comes Back Again; Creates Much Joy,' *Los Angeles Evening Express*, 2 March 1923, p.11.
34. 'Chaplin's Pilgrim Scorned by Clergy,' *Stevens Point Journal* [WI], 3 April 1923, p.1.
35. Edward G. Krief, 'Coast Film News,' *Variety*, 24 May 1923, p.18.
36. 'Cancels Chaplin Film at Request of Clergy,' *Exhibitors Herald*, 14 April 1923, p.42.

37. '[There has been a deal]', *Motion Picture News*, 5 May 1923, p.2151.
38. 'The Klan and "The Pilgrim,"' *Spartanburg* [SC] *Herald*, 28 April 1923, n. p.
39. '*Pilgrim* Passed When Will Hays Intervened,' *Exhibitors Herald*, 14 April, 1923, p.42, and 'Can You Imagine?' *Exhibitors Herald*, 4 March 1923, n. p.
40. 'Charlie in *Pilgrim* Is Not Barred,' *Los Angeles Times*, 11 March 1923, p.3.
41. 'Ohio Censor Cuts New Chaplin Film,' *Los Angeles Evening Post-Record*, 10 March 1923, p.8.
42. 'Pola Negris Tells of Meeting her "Dream Prince," of Love, Marriage and What Came to Her Afterward – Disillusionment, Unhappiness, and Divorce,' *San Francisco Chronicle*, 12 November 1922, p.3.
43. 'Charlie Chaplin to Marry Polish Actress, Report,' *Shreveport* [LA] *Journal*, 25 November 1922, p.4.
44. 'Pola Ends Betrothal; Chaplin Mends Break,' *Los Angeles Times*, 2 March, 1923, p.1.
45. Tilden would turn out to be an even worse choice. In November 1946 he was arrested for pedophilia and sentenced to a year in prison.
46. H.B.K. Willis, 'Pola Drops "Sharlie,"' *Los Angeles Times*, 28 July 1923, p.1, 3.
47. 'Closing Contract,' *Los Angeles Times*, 24 March 1922, p.27, and 'Miss Purviance Will Play in Comedies or Dramas,' *Los Angeles Times*, 1 February 1922, p.34.
48. 'Engaged? Charlie Chaplin Says "Nay, Nay," But Famous Film Star Talks of Women,' *San Francisco Chronicle*, 9 November 1922, p.13.
49. See Wes Gehring's *Charlie Chaplin and* A Woman of Paris, Jefferson, NC: McFarland & Co., 2021, Chapter 11.
50. Robinson, *Chaplin: His Life and Art*, Chapter 9.
51. 'After Shooting Continuity,' 1922, CHACHAA refers to Menjou's character as Letellier (also 'After Phone,' 1922) and Purviance's character is referred to as Peggy in 'After Kitchen,' 1922.
52. Adolphe Menjou was also a distant cousin of writer James Joyce.
53. 'Summary Analysis of *A Woman of Paris*; Production and Distribution, 1922. CHACHAA.
54. George W. Stark, 'Chaplin Here, A Notable Now,' no source, 15 October 1923, n. p.Pressbook. CHACHAA.
55. William C. Richards, 'Crowds Cheer Chaplin; Give Hoover "Go-By,"' *Detroit Free Press*, 16 October 1923, p.1, 3.

Epilogue: On into the Future: Chaplin's Remaining Life and Work

1. A synchronized soundtrack in 1931 is an orchestral track composed and performed to match the action and emotions portrayed onscreen.
2. The first film to utilize sound technology was, of course, Al Jolson's *The Jazz Singer* (1927).

3. "A Comedian Sees the World," in its published form, comprises five parts which appeared starting with the September 1933 issue of *Woman's Home Companion* (Crowell Publishing, Springfield, Ohio) and ending with the January 1934 issue. The managing editor for this series was Willa Roberts. From the primary documents available at CHACHAA, it can be ascertained that this series was largely Chaplin's own and as such it is perhaps the first instance of his own writing to appear in print, except for the 'economic policy' which he released to the papers on 27 June 1933 – a document which also resulted from the 1931–2 trip.

Bibliography

Books

Balio, Tino. *United Artists: The Company Built by Stars*. Madison, WI: U of WI P, 1976.

Chaplin, Charles. *My Trip Abroad*. New York, NY: Harper & Bros., 1922.

——. *My Autobiography*. London, UK: Bodley Head, 1964.

Gehring, Wes. *Charlie Chaplin and* A Woman of Paris, Jefferson, NC: McFarland & Co., 2021.

Goodwins, Fred. *Charlie Chaplin's Red Letter Days: At Work with the Comic Genius*. Ed. David James. Lanham, MD: Rowan & Littlefield, 2017.

Graham, Cooper C. and Christoph Irmscher, eds. *Love and Loss in Hollywood: Florence Deshon, Max Eastman and Charlie Chaplin*. Bloomington, IN: Indiana UP, 2021.

Haven, Lisa Stein. *The Rise and Fall of Max Linder: Cinema's First Celebrity*. Orlando, FL: BearManor Media, 2021.

Instone, Alfred. *Early Birds: Air Transport Memories 1919–1924*. Cardiff, Wales: *Western Mail & Echo*, 1938.

Maland, Charles J. *Chaplin and American Culture: The Evolution of a Star Image*. Princeton, NJ: Princeton UP, 1989.

Middleton, Kathleen M. *Bayonne*. Charleston, SC: Arcadia Publishing, 1995.

Robinson, David. *The Mirror of Opinion*. London, UK: Secker & Warburg, 1983.

——. *Chaplin: His Life and Art*. London, Penguin: 1985, 2001.

Stein, Lisa K. *Syd Chaplin: A Biography*. Jefferson, NC: McFarland & Co., 2010.

Periodicals

Architronic
Current Opinion
Early Popular Visual Culture
Exhibitor's Herald
Exhibitor's Trade Review
Film Culture
Financial History
Motion Picture

Motography
Moving Picture World
New York Review
Picture-Play
Pictures and Picture-goer
Pictures Press
Red Letter
Theatre
Trade Review
Variety
Wid's Daily

Newspapers
The Atlanta Constitution
Augusta Chronicle
Charleston [SC] *News-Courier*
Charlotte [NC] *Observer*
Chicago Tribune
Cleveland [OH] *Press*
The Columbia Record
The Commercial Appeal [Memphis, TN]
Courier-Journal [Louisville, KY]
The Daily Item [Port Chester, NY]
Daily News [NY, NY]
Dallas Times Herald
Des Moines [IA] *Sunday Register*
Deseret News [Salt Lake City, UT]
Detroit [MI] *Free Press*
The Dispatch [Lexington, NC]
The Evening Index [Greenwood, SC]
Evening Public Ledger [Philadelphia, PA]
The Evening Star [Washington, DC]
Evening Vanguard [Venice, CA]
Glasgow Bulletin
Greensboro [VA] *Daily News*
Harrisburg [PA] *Telegraph*
Hilo Daily Tribune
Honolulu Advertiser
Honolulu Star-Bulletin
Houston Post
Long Beach [CA] *Telegram*
Los Angeles Evening Citizen News

Los Angeles Evening Express
Los Angeles Evening Herald
Los Angeles Evening Post-Record
Los Angeles Times
Macon [GA] *Daily Telegraph*
Le Merle Blanc
Montgomery [AL] *Advertiser*
The Morning Telegraph [Washington, D.C.]
Nashville [TN] *Banner*
New York Herald
New York Mail
New York Review
New York Telegraph
New York Times
New York Tribune
News and Observer [Raleigh, NC]
News-Pilot [San Pedro, CA]
The Omaha [NE] *Daily Bee*
Pall Mall & Globe
Pasadena [CA] *Post*
Pomona [CA] *Progress Bulletin*
Salisbury [NC] *Evening Post*
Salt Lake City [UT] *Herald Republican*
Salt Lake [UT] *Telegram*
Salt Lake City [UT] *Tribune*
San Francisco [CA] *Chronicle*
San Francisco [CA] *Examiner*
Santa Ana [CA] *Register*
Shreveport [LA] *Journal*
Spartansburg [SC] *Herald*
Stevens Point [WI] *Journal*
Sunday Chronicle
The State [Columbia, SC]
Tacoma [WA] *News*
The Tennessean [Nashville, TN]
Times Dispatch [Richmond, VA]
Times-Picayune [New Orleans, LA]
Vancouver [BC, CANADA] *Daily World*
Whittier [CA] *News*
Winston-Salem [NC] *Journal*

Films

Chaplin, Charles, director. *A Dog's Life*. First National, 1918.
——. *Shoulder Arms*. First National, 1918.
——. *The Bond*. First National, 1918.
——. *Sunnyside*. First National, 1919.
——. *A Day's Pleasure*. First National, 1919.
——. *The Kid*. First National, 1921.
——. *The Idle Class*. First National, 1922.
——. *Pay Day*. First National, 1922.
——. *The Pilgrim*. First National, 1923.
——. *Woman of Paris*. United Artists, 1924.

Archives

Charlie Chaplin archive. Cineteca di Bologna, Bologna, Italy. Online database. Available online at charliechaplinarchive.org. CHACHAA.
Motion Picture Copyright Descriptions Collection, 1912–1977, Library of Congress, Washington, D.C. Available online at https://www.loc.gov/collections/motion-picture-copyright-descriptions/. LOC-MPCDC.
Rob Wagner Papers, 1925 to 1942, UCLA Library Special Collections, Charles E. Young Research Library. UCLA-SC-RWP.

Acknowledgements

No Chaplin book is possible without the graciousness and support of Kate Guyonvarch, directrice of Roy Export in Paris. Additional important supporters are Arnold Lozano, always helpful with photos and much more, also of Roy Export and soon to take over the helm in late 2022, Dominique Dugros, who I only wish I had given this manuscript to read before publication, because I know I will regret it, and supporters in spirit Uli Rūdel and Steve Massa. Of course, with a book like this, David Robinson was constantly looking over my shoulder. I felt his presence but tried very hard not to regurgitate his *Chaplin: His Life and Art* in this book and I think I mostly succeeded in that effort. Still, his influence and foundational knowledge on the topic is always important to my writing efforts.

My undying gratitude goes also to the caregivers of the charliechaplinarchive.org, the Cineteca di Bologna, without which this project would have been exceedingly more difficult and expensive to do, to Cecilia Cenciarelli and all the archivists there in Bologna responsible for scanning and creating the records for the database. Thanks to librarians Rebekah Scarborough-McGraw of the Genealogical and Historical Room and Kate Fisher, Head of Reference, both of the Middle Georgia Regional Library, and Suellyn Lathrop, Special Collections Archivist of Western Kentucky University for helping me to locate some hard-to-find articles. A huge thanks as always to mediahistoryproject.org, its founder David Pierce, current director Eric Hoyt and all other staff and contributors, for without this database, scholars of silent film would be significantly hampered in their ability to tell these important stories.

Index